Quiet Prayer

BOOKS BY MARIE CHAPIAN

FICTION
I Love You Like a Tomato

CHRISTIAN LIVING
Telling Yourself the Truth
with William Backus
*Why Do I Do What I Don't Want
to Do?* with William Backus
Love and Be Loved
Growing Closer
*Close Friends: Making
Them, Keeping Them*
Staying Happy in an Unhappy World
A Confident, Dynamic You
Angels in Our Lives
God in the Mirror with
Miles McPherson

BIOGRAPHIES
*The Emancipation of Robert
Sadler* with Robert Sadler
Help Me Remember, Help Me Forget
In the Morning of My Life
with Tom Netherton
Of Whom the World Was Not Worthy
Escape from Rage
Forgive Me with Cathy Crowell Webb
Back on Course with Gavin MacLeod
The Other Side of Suffering
with John Ramsey

Health and Fitness
Fun to Be Fit
Free to Be Thin with Neva Coyle
*The All-New Free to Be
Thin* with Neva Coyle
*Slimming Down and Growing
Up* with Neva Coyle

DEVOTIONALS
Heart for God
His Thoughts Toward Me
His Gifts Toward Me
Discovering Joy
Making His Heart Glad
The Secret Place of Strength
God's Heart For You
Talk to Me, Jesus: Devotional Journal
Talk to Me, Jesus: 365 Daily Devotions
Walk with Me, Jesus
*Am I the Only One Here
with Faded Genes?*
Feeling Small, Walking Tall

CHILDREN'S BOOKS
Mustard Seed Library for Children
Alula-Belle Button Top Paintbrush
Soft Shoe Pucheeni Magrew Books
*Harold and I, an Incredible
Journey of Supernatural Events*

Quiet Prayer

*The Hidden Purpose and Power
of Christian Meditation*

MARIE CHAPIAN

EMANATE
BOOKS

Published in Nashville, Tennessee, by Emanate Books, an imprint of Thomas Nelson. Emanate Books and Thomas Nelson are registered trademarks of HarperCollins Christian Publishing, Inc.

Thomas Nelson titles may be purchased in bulk for educational, business, fund-raising, or sales promotional use. For information, please e-mail SpecialMarkets@ThomasNelson.com.

Unless otherwise noted, Scripture quotations are taken from the New King James Version®. © 1982 by Thomas Nelson. Used by permission. All rights reserved.

Scripture quotations marked AMP are from the Amplified® Bible. Copyright © 1954, 1958, 1962, 1964, 1965, 1987 by The Lockman Foundation. Used by permission. (www.Lockman.org)

Scripture quotations marked AMPC are from the Amplified Bible, Classic Edition Copyright © 1954, 1958, 1962, 1964, 1965, 1987 by The Lockman Foundation.

Scripture quotations marked CEB are from the Common English Bible. Copyright © 2011 Common English Bible.

Scripture quotations marked GNT are from the Good News Translation in Today's English Version—Second Edition. Copyright 1992 by American Bible Society. Used by permission.

Scripture quotations marked KJV are from the King James Version. Public domain.

Scripture quotations marked NIV are from the Holy Bible, New International Version®, NIV®. Copyright © 1973, 1978, 1984, 2011 by Biblica, Inc.® Used by permission of Zondervan. All rights reserved worldwide. www.Zondervan.com. The "NIV" and "New International Version" are trademarks registered in the United States Patent and Trademark Office by Biblica, Inc.®

Scripture quotations marked RSV are from Revised Standard Version of the Bible. Copyright 1946, 1952, and 1971 National Council of the Churches of Christ in the United States of America. Used by permission. All rights reserved.

Scripture quotations marked TLV are from the Tree of Life Version.

Any Internet addresses, phone numbers, or company or product information printed in this book are offered as a resource and are not intended in any way to be or to imply an endorsement by Thomas Nelson, nor does Thomas Nelson vouch for the existence, content, or services of these sites, phone numbers, companies, or products beyond the life of this book.

ISBN 978-1-4002-1280-4 (eBook)
ISBN 978-1-4002-1275-0 (TP)

Library of Congress Control Number:2019947163

Printed in the United States of America

19 20 21 22 23   LSC   10 9 8 7 6 5 4 3 2 1

Contents

CONTENTS

CONTENTS

CONTENTS

Introduction

FOLLOWING THE DEATH OF CHRIST countless men and women fled to desert areas of Palestine, Egypt, Arabia, and Persia to live devout lives of prayer without persecution. The ancient Christian tradition of meditation began with these desert mothers (*ammas*) and fathers (*abbas*) who dedicated their lives to solitude and prayer. Churches, monasteries, convents, and religious orders were eventually formed, and the tradition of solitude and meditation prevailed within their hallowed walls. Confined to the daily life of the clergy in Orthodox and Catholic religions of the East and the West, the holy practice of prayer and meditation took the major portion of each day.

A popular but somewhat misleading definition of the ancient Christian meditation tradition has been that it's a discursive practice, meaning the study and pondering of the Word. The first psalm opens with "his delight is in the law of the LORD, and in His law he meditates day and night," which is pondering, studying, and thinking about the words on the page. Joshua also pondered the meaning, intent, and relevance of God's Word in his life as expressed in Joshua 1:8 where he proclaims that good success and prosperity are a result of meditation. Blessed is the person who studies the Word of God.

Quiet Prayer is nondiscursive meditation. In other words, it is meditation at its deepest, most profound, wordless level. Quiet Prayer Christian meditation is based on silence and stillness in the presence of God. We save pondering for our time of contemplation, or Bible study.

> But you, when you pray, go into your room, and when you have
> shut your door, pray to your Father who is in the secret place;
> and your Father who sees in secret will reward you openly.
> (Matthew 6:6)

Quiet Prayer is a child of Father Thomas Keating's Centering Prayer movement, of which I am a part. Quiet Prayer was born through devotion and love and a longing for a Protestant perspective of our ancient heritage.

Quiet Prayer is contemplative prayer. St. Teresa of Avila, born in 1515, described it this way: "Contemplative prayer in my opinion is nothing else than a close sharing between friends; it means taking time frequently to be alone with Him who we know loves us."[1]

Quiet Prayer meditation is the foundation of our contemplative life, and for the Christian life in general.

I consider myself a simple pilgrim on this inner journey with Jesus and meditation. I came to discover meditation without much of a background in any sort of meditation. I was unaware of any modern-day Protestant Christians who practiced meditation that could bring me closer to the heart of God. Of the hundreds of prayer meetings I'd been part of, not a single one was a quiet experience where nobody spoke or sat still for more than five minutes in silence enjoying God's presence.

The churches I was accustomed to weren't known for being particularly quiet in prayer or in worship, and the idea of meditation, if ever mentioned, was open for anyone's interpretation. It could be anything from dreaming of Elysian Fields while listening to soothing music or daydreaming about the streets of gold in heaven.

I was drawn to Christian meditation (Quiet Prayer) without any formal introduction. One evening in my writing studio several years ago, I was finishing up my day's work, and I heard very clearly these words coming from deep inside me: "Will you come and sit with Me for a while?" I knew immediately the Lord was calling me to quiet down and sit with Him. I obeyed and sat down. Quiet and still. I sat.

And sat. And sat. I made a habit of these quiet times sitting with Him. Daily. As I told you, I didn't know anything about Christian meditation, but I remembered that I had been asking God for a deeper walk with Him.

In the following days and months I studied the Bible to learn what it had to teach about meditation prayer, and I also researched the ancient Christian tradition of meditation. I studied writings of the desert mystics, the saints, monks, nuns, and the modern-day monastic Thomas Merton. I could find almost nothing on the practice of nondiscursive meditation in the Protestant tradition.

I traveled to Catholic contemplative prayer retreats and events across the United States. I enrolled in one- and two-year programs in contemplative studies and became a facilitative Centering Prayer leader.

It began with these simple words, "Will you sit with Me for a while?"

Now, several years later, I share with you the practice of Quiet

Prayer not only through my own life's experience, but through the culmination of what I've learned from the great Christian masters, saints, mystics, and practitioners of Christian meditation both ancient and contemporary.

Quiet Prayer won't replace other forms of prayer. It's in addition to our times of imprecation, adoration, worship, praise, and intercession, including our daily Bible study. It's the process of shifting from whatever level of spiritual awareness we are at to a deeper experience of the presence of God at the core of us.

The world around us teems with chaos, turmoil, and noise. We can change the turmoil of the world around us by first changing the turmoil within us. That's exactly what Quiet Prayer and this book is all about.

WE CAN CHANGE

THE TURMOIL

OF THE WORLD

AROUND US BY FIRST

CHANGING THE

TURMOIL WITHIN US.

In the Beginning

If you're seeking a deeper relationship with Jesus, let me share what I've learned from soaring on the wings of meditation. I have learned that meditation, or Quiet Prayer, is something I can't live without.

I know the feeling of wanting more of God, of craving a deeper, richer relationship with Him. I know what it's like to live in a world surrounded by unbelievers when my spiritual life had to be kept private and my praise and worship kept solo. But I also know what it's like to live within a twenty-four-hour ministry life surrounded by Christians and Christian workers, activities, and service. In fact, for most of my adult life I have served God full-time in ministry as an author, teacher, conference speaker, and counselor.

It's not what we do that enlarges our spirits or brings us closer to God. It's not what we do that brings us inner peace either. I've never known anyone who doesn't want, even long for, inner peace in their lives. Inner peace is a deep, deep life experience that takes practice. Though it's a gift of the Spirit, like love and patience, it can remain distant and elusive. It has to be lived. Who doesn't crave inner peace? Have you ever met anyone who enjoys being anxious, nervous, sleepless, fearful, worried, judgmental, moody, irritable, controlling, bitter, and eventually suffering from heart, liver, circulation, and digestive diseases?

We have the mistaken idea that God is outside us and that His gifts and answered prayers somehow depend on His opening His almighty hand and dropping them down on us from on high.

We see ourselves separate from the God who loves us and sent His Son to die for us. It's the shallow spirit that begs God for what it already possesses.

Our desire for peace and more of God is prompted by the Holy Spirit. Such desires are truly holy. A person who doesn't give a hoot about God may still crave inner peace, but you, child of God, are on an altogether different track. Four times the following words are repeated in the Gospels: "Jesus looked at them and said, 'With people [as far as it depends on them] it is impossible, but with God all things are possible'" (Matthew 19:26 AMP).

We wait for inner peace to sweep over us when things in our lives are going exceptionally well. *I don't get it*, we might wonder. *How come I can't sleep?* The answer I offer is, inner peace takes inner transformation and is not contingent on circumstances, situations, or relationships. Even a relatively peaceful life doesn't promise inner peace. Some of the most stressed, moody, and needy people you'll meet will be people living in the cozy lap of luxury and leisure.

If you'd love to have true inner peace reigning in your life, and you're a child of God, read on.

Every now and then a conscientious Christian soul will confide, "If I get too close to God, I'm afraid He'll want me to give up stuff—you know, surrender all. Suppose He wants me to be a missionary someplace like Siberia in fifty-below-zero weather."

I laugh out loud. Siberia. Actually, years ago when I dreamed of becoming a missionary, I worried I'd be sent off to the Arctic to live on whale fat and search for lost Inuits.

God is no dictator. Our fears can be dictators in our lives, however. God cares about our wants and desires. You'll discover through Quiet Prayer that your desires actually line up with His. What a relief to learn when I was in my twenties that God had things perfectly under control in the frozen Arctic and didn't need me there at all.

Other seemingly normal Christian people have revealed their hesitancy to engage in Quiet Prayer meditation because, and I quote, "I shouldn't sit here quietly, I should be out there on the prayer battlefield with my sword in hand, waging war for the sake of the kingdom of God! Just look at the state of the world!"

What could I say?

If your suggestion is that I advise the person to add Quiet Prayer alongside the intercessory and other prayers of the day, that's what I did. He seemed okay with it and not long after joined a Quiet Prayer group.

Quiet Prayer is a means of solidly fusing our human spirits to the Holy Spirit as we focus on Jesus. It sounds so simple, and in reality it is simple, yet it's also not so simple.

Ask yourself this question: If God is in me, how will I find Him there?

IT'S THE

SHALLOW SPIRIT

THAT BEGS

GOD FOR WHAT

IT ALREADY

POSSESSES.

Quiet Prayer Session

IT'S A FINE AUTUMN MORNING AND FOUR OF US SIT together in a room with windows all around. The person on my right reads aloud from the Bible on her cell phone: "He who dwells in the secret place of the Most High shall abide in the shadow of the Almighty," and we're all quiet. The only sound is the jostle of the tree branches outside the window. A few leaves flutter in the gentle autumn wind.

"I love Psalm 91," someone says.

"Me too," says another. "My favorite."

Then someone asks, "What's the secret place?"

Two people respond, "Secret means in private!"

Another says, "I think it means where God lives."

I smile because they are each right. Partially right, that is.

"The secret place is where He lives in you," I offer.

The sound of tree branches against the window. No one fidgets or speaks. Three pairs of eyes are fixed on me.

These are evangelical Christians. Churchgoers. Good people. They're interested in what Quiet Prayer is all about and indicated they could hardly wait to "try it out." I explain to them that Quiet Prayer is a way of life. It affects every molecule of us and is not like other forms of prayer.

Quiet Prayer is in addition to other forms of prayer that we're accustomed to, I explain. It does not take their place. Quiet prayer is a set-apart, purposeful time to enter the secret place of the Most High and just sit with God. It's a time and place where there are no words but simply the experience of sitting still with God in His presence while saying nothing, asking nothing, as we set aside our wants and desires.

In these short and timed moments we make the choice to calm our busy minds and focus on Jesus and His presence with us and in us.

I explain there's a place for intercession, praise and worship, adoration, inquiry, recitation, chanting, singing, dancing in the Spirit, praying in tongues, signs, wonders, and visions. But Quiet Prayer is different. Here you sit in stillness in God's presence, and nothing else. It's a designated time to concentrate on and absorb God's presence.

To prepare for our period of meditation today we selected and read a portion of Scripture (the entire ninety-first Psalm) and we're now quieting ourselves in preparation for stillness. The words we just read swirl around us and embrace us. Outside it begins to rain but nobody notices.

"Say, Marie," whispers the woman on my left. "Would you mind visiting my sick aunt? She's in really bad shape."

"Of course," I whisper back.

I gently sound the bell to start the timer and begin our practice. The rain becomes a full orchestra outside. I close my eyes and listen. When I open them twenty minutes later, I see three pairs of eyes closed.

We meet again the following week. There's coffee brewing and a pot of mint tea waiting. The rain has brought cooler weather and we sit in heavy sweaters. A new person has joined us and we are now five.

"I don't know if I'm able to do Quiet Prayer," says the new person. "I find it very hard to concentrate or sit still." She demonstrated by bouncing on the chair and giggling.

"Welcome!" I respond, smiling. "How wonderful. You'll do just great."

In my experience I've noted the ones who say they can't concentrate do just fine in contemplative prayer. They know from the get-go that there's a challenge ahead and they go for it. Once the peace of God captures the soul there's no turning back.

For any of us.

"And another thing," says the woman. "I already meditate."

"I'm delighted to hear it," I tell her.

"I sit and talk to Jesus every day. In fact I talk to Him all day long," she says.

"That's wonderful," I tell her.

She gives me a look. I can tell she's waiting for me to correct her idea of meditation.

I smile and sip my coffee. "God loves it when we give ourselves to Him. How wonderful that you talk to Him all day long."

"Yes," she says, with a hint of mutiny in her voice, "that's how I meditate and I have visions! The Lord appears to me!"

"That's beautiful," I tell her.

The others look pleased.

"It's important for us to know there's no right or wrong when it comes to our personal modes of prayer," I tell them. "Our new person has brought up something important. There are endless ways to pray. God honors them all. I like to pray while swimming laps in the local pool. I don't count laps by number but by verses.

We pray while running, driving, waiting, flying; we pray in all places at all times. The Bible tells us to 'pray without ceasing,' and what better way than talking to God all day long no matter what we're doing or where we are?

"Quiet Prayer is different from most forms of prayer because it's silent meditation without the use of words. We focus on Jesus Christ in silence. We pass no judgment on others or on ourselves."

The new person looks more relaxed.

The woman to my right leans over to me, obviously worried about something.

"Marie—"

I turn and face her, concerned maybe something is hurting her.

"You haven't visited my aunt yet!"

Her aunt.

"Oh yes. Yes, of course." My voice is oddly not reassuring.

"She's getting worse, Marie. Please."

"Yes, yes, of course."

I ask her to read our Scripture verse, Matthew 6:6:

But you, when you pray, go into your room, and when you have shut your door, pray to your Father who is in the secret place; and your Father who sees in secret will reward you openly.

PART 1

Into the Quiet

Stillness waits for you.

Peace longs for you.

Love reaches for you.

Is It Christian to Meditate?

THE HISTORY OF CHRISTIAN MEDITATION BEGINS with Jesus Himself as we see Him withdraw to quiet places for solitude with God (Luke 5:16). John the Baptist, after the death of his mother, Elizabeth, took permanent residence in the desert region of the Dead Sea for prayer and solitude with God (Matthew 3:1–12). John the Baptist could possibly be considered Christianity's first hermit monk—a selfless man living alone and owning nothing, a Nazarite Jew dedicated to loving and serving God, and finally, through that profound love, leading others, baptizing, and proclaiming the kingship of the King of kings, the awaited-for Messiah, Jesus Christ (Luke 5:16).

The apostle Paul withdrew into the desert of Arabia for three years to pray, hear from God, and learn of the Savior whose voice spoke to him on the Damascus road. The time spent separated from the noise and chaos of the world prepared him for his ministry as the great apostle of Christ he was to become. He took himself to the Sinai Peninsula where Moses received the Ten Commandments, drawn by the same Holy Spirit who had driven Elijah to that region. "I conferred not with flesh and blood . . . , but I went into Arabia" (Galatians 1:16–17 KJV). In solitude Paul's spirit became one with God's Holy Spirit and he was transformed.

Many of the earliest followers of Christ chose to leave their active, busy lives in the world to live in cloistered cells and caves as hermits and anchorites of the desert. These men and women of God called *abbas* and *ammas*, fathers and mothers of the faith, were looked up to as spiritual guides, mentors, healers, and deliverers in their time.

How did these early believers live? In the first century AD, Philo of Alexandria (c. 25 BC to c. AD 50) described a Jewish ascetic community of men and women on the shores of Lake Mareotis in the vicinity of Alexandria, Egypt. Members of the community lived apart from one another during the six days of the week, studying the Hebrew Bible (the Tanakh) during the daytime and eating at evening. Members of the community composed books of Midrash, an allegorical method for interpreting Scripture. Only on the Sabbath would they meet and share their learning, eat a common meal of bread and spring water, and listen to a lecture on the Torah. Every seventh Sabbath was accorded a festival of learning, singing, and dancing. These were Jews who found Christ. Remember the early believers were predominantly Hebrew.

What Is Quiet Prayer Meditation?

SIMPLE. I'VE ALREADY INDICATED QUIET PRAYER IS a form of Christian meditation updated from ancient times where we bring ourselves into the presence of God in stillness. We bring ourselves into the presence of God's love, which is perfect and complete, and which we can't begin to fathom with our itsy-bitsy mortal minds. This is why silence is so powerful when meditating. When we quiet our minds and stop utilizing words during these moments alone with Him, we can enter into the presence of God with who we are, not who we think we are, or what we've done or not done, or what we think we want, but just who we are at this moment.

Stripped of wordy descriptions or explanations of ourselves, we humbly bring all of who we are to all of who Jesus is. We gently slip into who He is and into His presence, freeing ourselves from the cares we carry with us 24/7.

Quiet Prayer is a set-apart time to make our entrance into our personal, private holy place with the holy One, the mighty One, the immortal One, the Father Almighty who loves us.

You'll notice in this book I use the names of God and Jesus interchangeably. I don't pause to identify God the Father and Jesus the Son, but refer to them as One. You'll read, "Focus on Jesus" and "Focus on God," so together we can experience the vastness of the Godhead through the Holy Spirit.

The Practice of Quiet Prayer

LET'S PAUSE HERE TO GIVE YOU THE OPPORTUNITY to engage in the first Quiet Prayer Practice in this book.

Let's take a minute or so to prepare.

As you prepare for the first of four sessions of Quiet Prayer in this book, consider for a moment that when you set your timer and close your eyes, you'll be entering the intimate presence of God in a new way. As a Christian you're with Him all day, of course, but your Quiet Prayer time is a purposeful set-apart time of intense focus and intimacy.

As soon as you close your eyes, your mind will inevitably erupt with a volcano of thoughts. Not to fret. It's natural. In fact, it's the ordinary state of your busy, busy mind. Call it mind clutter, the jillion thoughts that fly across the open field of your mind like colonies of bees.

Before falling to the rocky shoals of confusion, know that in these moments of meditation the Holy Spirit works in you, restoring you to your true spiritual self, your higher self. You sit in obedience and He gently slips you out of your inner conflicts and opens your spirit to knowing Him beyond anything your human mind can dream up.

If you can embrace the holy Quiet Prayer experience of the Holy Spirit vibrating within your spirit, and if you can sit in stillness with your spirit filled with His, you'll know what needs no words. Transformation has begun.

QUIET PRAYER PRACTICE #1

I INVITE YOU TO SHARE WITH ME THE PRACTICE OF Quiet Prayer as I've outlined below. Not as a list of rules, I offer the practice as a pattern to follow on your beautiful contemplative path. (More on the contemplative path later.)

The format I've presented below has proven to be successful in groups and for solo use, but please feel free to modify your practice to fit your need.

Begin with reading a portion of Scripture to bring your mind and heart to the Lord.

John 14:25–27 is one suggestion:

These things I have spoken to you while being present with you. But the Helper, the Holy Spirit, whom the Father will send in My name, He will teach you all things, and bring to your remembrance all things that I said to you. Peace I leave with you, My peace I give to you; not as the world gives do I give to you. Let not your heart be troubled, neither let it be afraid.

1. *Sit in a nice, comfortable upright position, feet flat on the floor with your hips, shoulders, and ears in alignment.* Relax the muscles of your neck, shoulders, and face. Place your hands loosely settled on your lap.

(Note: You may prefer to sit cross-legged on a cushion, sofa, chair, or on the ground. Sit upright with your hips, shoulders, and ears in alignment. Hands loosely settled on your lap.)

2. *Take a few deep breaths.* Breathe in slowly and evenly. Breathe out slowly and evenly. Sense your body refreshed and cleansed as you take in and release each breath. Allow all cares to spiral out of you with each outward breath.

3. *Select a special sacred word or short verse from the Bible.* You'll use this to help brush away those pesky thoughts that crop up as you sit. Make it simple, just a few words. Your sacred word is your friend and will help to quiet your busy mind.

Silently brush aside mental intrusions with your chosen sacred word. Quieting the untrained, unbridled mind is the major work of meditation. Silently speak your sacred word as you brush aside a thought and then return your focus to God.

4. *Ring a little bell to begin and end your practice.* I sometimes play a minute or two of soft meditative music or Gregorian chant on my cell phone at the beginning and end of each session.

(Note: Other inviting sounds are a tinkling bell or gentle chime—just so it's not shrill or brash sounding like a schoolyard whistle or the buzzer of a clothes dryer.)

5. *As you begin your set-apart time, sound the bell to declare this time is devoted to the Lord.* It's the signal that invites you to enter your sacred space with God, much like a church bell calling the people to worship.

6. You may choose to read aloud the portion of Scripture here. Read slowly. Pause for a few seconds and then repeat the Scripture if you wish.

7. You sounded the bell once, announcing this holy period of time, and the reading of the Word. *Now sound the bell again to enter your actual Quiet Prayer.* Gently close your eyes as a

loving act of intention. You're closing your eyes to the outward environment to remain focused inwardly on God.

8. *Sit alert, yet with no tension in the body as you begin to focus your attention on God Himself in the person of Jesus Christ.* For the next twenty minutes you have nowhere to go, nothing to do, no stress or duties assail you; you are simply alone in silence with God, who loves you. Remember your sacred word to silently brush away intrusive thoughts and return your focus on the Lord Jesus.

9. At the sound indicating the close of your Quiet Prayer session, you may want to remain still for a longer period. In that case *reset your timer.* (It's important to always use a timer for your meditation sessions. It keeps you centered and focused.)

10. *Sound the bell again at the close, this time three times.* One, to indicate the close of this period of meditation; two, to gently open your eyes and return to your day; and three, to breathe your thankfulness.

That's the basic bones of Quiet Prayer practice. Later in this book you'll advance with additional suggested practice sessions as well as a simple one-minute practice. We'll look into the deepest aspects of Quiet Prayer, why it's transformative, and how it affects our lives in a permanent way.

Quiet Prayer is . . .

In this place for these minutes

    you haven't a care in the world.

You have nowhere to go, nothing to do.

You haven't a single responsibility,

    not a single duty to perform.

In this place for these minutes

    all that exists is you and God.

Nothing else.

There's nobody to please,

    no pressures to do anything at all.

No past, no future,

    only here in this space with God

    right now.

What if you don't have ten or twenty minutes for Quiet Prayer?

On those days give to God what's possible for you. Any time spent alone and focused on God is better than none. Again, don't confuse Quiet Prayer with your other prayer times. Other forms of prayer use words. Quiet Prayer is silent and wordless, calling for intense focus on God alone during a designated period of time.

God fits His Holy Spirit into your spirit. He measures your capacity for His divine presence to fit comfortably into your openness to Him. This is what happens in the popular expression, "God meets us right where we are." He doesn't charge through closed doors of your heart or insist you receive more of Him than you're ready for. That's like God offering you a healthy, organic farm-fresh meal when you're already stuffed to the max on beef jerky and ice cream. No, God in His excessive kindness enters into the space we give Him.

God won't withhold Himself when invited. When you open yourself to Jesus and His presence in Quiet Prayer, He meets you right where you are. "Call on Me and I will answer," He has said, and "Knock and it will be opened," and "Come unto Me, all you who labor and are heavy laden." He is always calling to you to open your spirit to His. Why? Because He wants a deeper relationship with you just like you want with Him.

God wants to be more than the love of your life.

Years ago a student of mine gave me a book called *In the Spirit of Happiness*, written by contemporary Orthodox monks who believe that human beings were created to be happy. These men believe that the elements of a monk's life—self-discipline, solitude, prayer, acts of love, and forgiveness—are the pathways to achieve true happiness that anyone can follow. They wrote:

> God cannot fill what's already filled with itself. He can only fill us to the extent that we let go of ourselves so He can fill us with Himself.[1]

The first-century abbas and ammas in the desert were well acquainted with the joy of the Lord. Christians with foundations in meditation joyfully experienced their callings. Not all monks, priests, nuns, and public believers were solemn, half-starved monastics, as we tend to think of them. For the most part these early practitioners of meditation and contemplation were a joyful lot with an aura of peace and humility about them. They sang, danced, and praised God with great delight.

The early abbas and ammas schooled their anchorites in the Scriptures and holy, self-sacrificial living based on solitude and meditation. Today when you sit in Quiet Prayer, consider your predecessors who sat just like you, in holy union with God.

The desert abbas and ammas were men and women of extreme discipline. They didn't lie around outside their cells in the rocks all day, chewing on weeds and sunbathing. In the desert they had to build their cells by hand, carrying water and making bricks. Water is necessary to survive, so many built their cells or cave-like hermitages near the river. They also dug wells in the Wadi Nahum that produced salty water.

The monk and theologian John Cassian (360–435) included in his writings the accounts of the monks who chose more solitude and therefore built their cells farther from water. One monk who spent ninety years in the desert had purposely built his cell five miles from the first desert church and water. Each Sunday after the service he could be seen hauling on his back the water he needed for the week. When he was told he should move closer to the wells, he moved five miles farther away.[2]

Other anchorites chose to live thirty and forty miles from water and each Sunday after church carried on their backs their week's supply of water back to their cell.

Things that we consider absolutely necessary, like running water, the desert fathers would consider a laughable luxury. One anchorite told Cassian, and I'll paraphrase, "We could have set our cells on the banks of the Nile and had water at our doors. We could set ourselves on more fertile land and grow lush gardens for plentiful food. But we despise these luxuries. We scorn them along with all the pleasures of the world, and delight in the dreadful and vast desert. No amount of riches can compare to these barren sands."

The hours spent alone with God with no interruptions, hindrances, or outward disturbances were the greatest joy in life. In fact it was their lives' pursuit and purpose. Their hard labor and severity of living conditions seemed a joyful privilege.

They were happy. They had two clay cups in their cells, one for themselves and one for guests. These people weren't psychotic weirdos with hairy bodies, muttering and drooling into their beards. No, many were educated and born into wealth. For the most part, they were hospitable, very kind people. They helped newcomers build their cells, they shared their bread, and they encouraged one another. Of course there were also those who chose total, isolated solitude.

These are the Christian fathers and mothers who led the path for us in our intimate daily journeys into the intimate presence of Jesus through silence and meditation.

Have patience with everything unresolved in

    your heart

        and try to love the questions

           themselves . . .

Don't search for the answers,

        which could not be given to you now,

        because you would not be able to live

          them.

And the point is, to live everything.

Live the questions now.

Perhaps then, someday far in the future,

        you will gradually, without even noticing it,

        live your way into the answer.[3]

           —Rainer Maria Rilke

Visit

THE WOMAN IN THE BED HAS BEEN SICK FOR WEEKS. "Did my niece send you?"

"She's concerned for you."

"I know. Is that a Bible you've got there? Did you come to give me Last Rites?"

I smile.

"I came to offer life," I tell her.

In the next hour I learn that she belonged to a church that had her on their prayer list since she took sick. She had been a deaconess. She says if God exists, He's out of reach. She heard about Quiet Prayer from her niece, but doesn't think it's for her.

"What did you mean when you said you came to offer me life?"

We sit in the dark, humid room, I on a straight chair by the partially raised bed, and she propped up with a couple of pillows with her free hand reaching toward mine.

I look around at the room with its bare walls except for a religious calendar and a small wooden cross hanging by the closet. Curtains cover the one window in the room casting filmy, gray shadows on the floor.

"Do you think it's cold in here?" she asks. "I'm always cold," she adds. "God is punishing me."

She tells me about herself; she's been a Christian all her life but doesn't think she ever knew God or Jesus, and this has been bothering her lately. "When I was young I led a wild life even though I went to church. God's getting back at me now with all these physical problems. I guess I had way too much fun for Him."

Her poor joke falls flat when she sees the serious expression on my face. I'm thinking it'll take more than one visit to help her see how God longs to be her friend.

What keeps us from intimacy with God? Right up at the top of the list is not forgiving ourselves for whatever separates us from Him.

How can we believe we're loved unconditionally by God, as the Bible claims, if we can't forgive, let go of the past, and trust Him with our lives? Can we love God if our hearts are filled with self-imposed shame? Guilt? Unconscious self-loathing? Why can't we see ourselves as God sees us?

"God's finished with me," she says, turning her face.

I hear the hollowness in her voice. She speaks from what Thomas Merton called the Lower Self, or "False Self," where faith is never deep or relational. It's dysfunctional because basically it thrives on a nonspiritual human level. If the believer is going through the motions—doing good works, being a good person, and even serving in ministry—their work depends on their human abilities.

"I feel empty inside," the sick woman suddenly cries, grabbing my hand. "I'm bored, empty, and sick of being sick!"

She's looking for answers. In spite of her brokenness, I see she's desperately seeking God. I give her my other hand and begin to pray aloud. Her hands tremble in mine. The presence of the Lord embraces us. He has the answers for her.

The Higher and Lower Self

WE ALL NEED TO RECOGNIZE OUR HIGHER SELF. Our Higher Self, or our True Self, is that part of us that reflects the bright luminosity of God Himself in us. It's the truth of who we are.

Your Higher Self is your True Self. It's who you were born to be.

Your Lower Self, or False Self, is that part of you the Bible calls the "flesh," monumentally selfish and fighting for independence from God's will. The False Self is concerned with Self. Period.

The uncertainty and the troubles of the world tempt us to grasp onto anything that relieves pain, making us easy targets for flattery, false promises, and disappointment. The False Self thinks nothing of selfishly ordering God around, telling Him what to do, and calling it prayer.

The Lower Self, or the False Self, is ruled by the ego. Our egos are only concerned with self. Our egos love to impress others and, if we consider ourselves religious, to impress God. Quiet Prayer calms the ego; and when it pops up during Quiet Prayer, you'll recognize it by your self-aggrandizing thoughts where you're always the hero. Your ego hates resting in God because you can't *do* something. It's your ego that wants to tell God what to do, not the other way around.

It's the dominance of the ego, the False Self, who wants people to see how spiritual you are. Your Higher Self is thrilled and content as a mere pilgrim traveling on a lifetime journey of humility before God and the world.

It's your ego, or False Self, that demands recognition for your good deeds. It's your ego, or False Self, that's inflexible, controlling, proud, and judgmental.

The Lower Self, no matter how peppy and smart, is in a steely, spiritual slumber. The Lower Self sleepwalks in the glorious light of God. Paul warned the Romans to wake up. He told them to put their lives in the Lord Jesus Christ while there was still time and to "make no provision for the flesh." He was referring directly to the Lower Self with that word *flesh*. Make no provision for your Lower Self to mess up your life.

Let's give these verses a closer look:

> The night is far spent, the day is at hand. Therefore let us cast off the works of darkness [Lower Self], and let us put on the armor of light [Higher Self]. Let us walk properly, as in the day, not in revelry and drunkenness, not in lewdness and lust, not in strife and envy. But put on the Lord Jesus Christ, and make no provision for the flesh, to fulfill its lusts. (Romans 13:11–14)

Did you notice that strife and envy are equally named right along with drunkenness, lewdness, and lust? Ouch. Strife and envy are Lower Self traits, and the Higher Self works to "make no provision" for its egoist lusts. Your Higher Self works at not giving a thought to gratifying the flesh and its selfish desires.

Augustine, the famous Christian theologian and saint, whose writings influenced the development of Western Christianity, was painfully aware of his ego (Lower Self). He complained to God that his ego "dragged him away" in moments of trying to hear from Him.

The ego thrives on religious legalism and aims to do better than others at making the grade at righteousness. *Integrity* is a word the ego defines as "control." The False Self is all about control. The ego is miserable when out of control.

During Quiet Prayer your Higher Self ignores the ego and its demands for attention and tosses it into the back seat. During the humble, loving consent and discipline of Quiet Prayer, the ego is deprived of its control. Quiet Prayer cleanses the False Self and its prickly ego. Daily meditating in the presence of God is spiritually cleansing, and over time sin no longer has the stronghold it once had on us. Second Corinthians 5:17 becomes our reality:

> Therefore, if anyone is in Christ, he is a new creation; old things have passed away; behold, all things have become new.

We won't become completely sinless until we stop breathing, but in recognizing our False Self and ego, we can choose to quickly employ our Spirit-filled power of the Higher Self into the situation. We have more inner power than we know.

Consider this:

Are you beginning to recognize how Quiet Prayer reaches into the very core of who you are?

Attach the words "because I love God" to everything you do and see what happens.

Do you know the price of surrender?

Think of the children's song, "This little light of mine, I'm gonna let it shine."

How little is your light?

The Father, Son, and Holy Spirit are intimate with you because you've made the holy Trinity's love the focus of your life.

Living out a life of love for God takes courage. You're far more courageous than you think.

Let's venture over to John 15. Jesus loved to use symbology and metaphor in His teaching, and here He used the symbols of the vine and branch to make His point. He began by establishing His position with the gardener, God the Father: "I am the real vine, and my Father is the gardener" (GNT).

A branch of a tree can't exist without its attachment to the tree (the vine). It's the only way it can thrive because it can't get nourishment anywhere else. Jesus followed the illustration in exquisitely plain language: "Without Me you can do nothing" (John 15:5).

Jesus went further and told us not only to become one with Him but to remain one with Him. The word *abide* means "to remain." Persist. Stay put. Don't budge. Be resolute, unmovable, permanently fixed.

We are to stay permanently fixed to Him because day-by-day He flourishes in greater and greater measure in us. His Spirit surges through the blood in our veins flourishing, blossoming, blooming, bursting forth with fruit, and you and I, His permanently fixed little branches, lack absolutely nothing. We are complete in Him. This is what Paul referred to when he wrote in Colossians 2:10 that we are "complete in [Christ]" or, as the NIV phrases it, we are "brought to fullness."

Jesus wants us to get it into our spirits that as branches securely connected to the Vine, we're complete; we have everything we need. We're complete in the One "who is the head of all principality and power" (Colossians 2:10).

This divine connection doesn't do well if we don't work at staying connected. If a branch becomes haphazardly attached to the tree, eventually it dries up, falls off, and clutters the floor of the forest. The practice of Quiet Prayer zeros us right into that state of permanence. It is connection at the highest level, because the work of our intense focus on Jesus in meditation tightens our union with Him where it can only flourish.

We can't abide, or remain permanently fixed, if we're loosely connected. You'll know when you need to work on tightening up your oneness with the Vine by your attitudes and the choices you make, because in Christ we lack nothing. What does that mean to you? Think of all the things we're taught to believe we need in order to live a good life—possessions, physical attractiveness, luxurious vacations, prestigious awards. These are fine, but all are secondary to our single major need, and when this is fulfilled, we're complete and we know it. From this place of fullness, "all things work together for good" (Romans 8:28) because we're permanently attached to Jesus, the head of all principality and authority (Colossians 2:10), and we're in love, completely in love with Jesus, with or without contingencies.

We're called according to His purpose and we can "do all things through Christ" (Philippians 4:13) because we're permanently fixed to His strength that flows through our veins.

I paraphrased a bit, but think for a minute. God has shown us a means to tighten up our attachment to Him, and that's through meditation, or Quiet Prayer.

GOD HAS SHOWN US

A MEANS TO TIGHTEN

UP OUR ATTACHMENT

TO HIM, AND THAT'S

THROUGH MEDITATION,

OR QUIET PRAYER.

We pray for needs to be met, for safety, for health, for prosperity, but if these prayers are not from the place of oneness like the branch and the tree, it's as if we're asking favors from someone we don't know very well. It stands to reason that if we're intimately one with God, and we know Him, we know His will, how He thinks, what pleases Him, what His desires are, what He forbids, what He expects of us, not to mention that He is all power, majesty, and glory (I could write a book). He reveals Himself to us as we daily read His Word, pray, and meditate. He wants us to know Him.

Understand that Jesus was talking about us as His spiritual children. He emphasized the only way to know Him is on His terms (John 15). As eternal beings we unite with Him who is eternity itself. He has chosen an invisible spiritual union with us to be the only way to know Him. He made that quite clear with, "I am the way, the truth, and the life" (John 14:6). We're transformed inwardly when these words take over our spirits.

You can see now that bearing fruit for God isn't a matter of white-knuckling, doing work we don't want to do, and racking up good deeds. "Live in Me and I will live in you" is what He's trying to get across to us. It's from this inner union that our prayers derive because "no branch can bear fruit of itself" (AMPC).

It takes effort and time to grasp the full implications of Jesus' words in John 15. I think I've read that chapter more than a hundred times and it's still new to me. Consistent Quiet Prayer practice helps to bring the reality of Jesus' words into my spirit and tighten my connection to Him as my lifeblood.

Let's drink in these words of Jesus: "I have told you this so that

My joy may be in you and that your joy may be complete" (John 15:11 NIV). There's that word *complete* again.

I suggest a very slow, concentrated reading of John 15. Contemplate the words; absorb them into your spirit. Follow your reading with a twenty-minute session of Quiet Prayer and focus entirely on Jesus and your complete union with Him.

As time goes by and your Quiet Prayer practice becomes as natural to you as breathing, your branch becomes more and more beautiful. Your beauty is His beauty. God's Holy Spirit in you brings you to new spiritual heights and the words "If you remain in Me and My words remain in you, ask whatever you wish, and it will be done for you" will never be far away again. You and the promises of God are one.

St. Antony of the Desert

St. Antony of the Desert, also called St. Anthony the Great (AD 251–356), always gave his favorite recommendation: "to be joyful at all times." Knowing they were forgiven of even the most grue-some sins, his disciples must have demonstrated the enthusiasm and elation in Christ that they shared. Observers said, "We could see them exulting in the desert to such an extent that nowhere on earth could one find such jubilation, such physical contentment."[1]

Years later St. Anthony of Padua (1195–1231) became a leg-endary example of the influence of the ascetic life. He chose to withdraw to the most remote and hazardous area of the Egyptian desert. Although he lived in solitude, his spiritual influence was acclaimed and sought after by people as far away as Spain, Gaul, Rome, and England.[2]

Anthony was thirty-five years old when he left society to live a life of solitude. He crossed the Nile, and on a mountain near the east bank, now called Der el Memun, he found an old fort where he shut himself inside. He lived there for twenty years without seeing another human being. Food was thrown to him over the wall.

Gradually other ascetics moved into caves and huts near Anthony's mountain, and a colony of followers was formed who continually called out to him, begging him to guide them in the spiritual life. In the year 305, he finally submitted and emerged from his retreat. To the amazement of all, he appeared to be exactly as when he had gone in, not emaciated, but vigorous in body and mind. He stayed with them a while and then again retreated to the mountain where he spent the last forty-five years of his life in seclusion.

What Is Contemplation?

CONTEMPLATION IS THE STUDY OF GOD'S WORD; it's thinking about it, praying about it, asking how it applies to our lives and the world today, and how we can make the Word alive in our daily lives as well as the world.

If we believe without question the opening verses of the Gospel of John, we know we're ingesting God Himself when we study His Word (John 1:1).

> In the beginning [before all time] was the Word (Christ), and the Word was with God, and the Word was God Himself. (AMP)

For Christianity's first sixteen centuries, contemplative prayer and meditation flourished at the heart and core of Christian spirituality. From the tradition of prayer and meditation during the time of the Old Testament prophets to the days of Jesus and following with the lives of the desert ammas and abbas through the Reformation and the end of the seventeenth century, meditation and contemplation were foundational to the faith walk.

Unfortunately after the years following the Reformation, the practice of meditation began to be de-emphasized in monasteries in the West, and it wasn't until the twentieth century that Christian meditation in the lives of everyday lay believers, as well as clergy, emerged and began to bloom.

Quiet Prayer is one modern-day name for this sacred and

transforming practice of meditating on Christ in stillness and holy desire.

There are many other traditions of meditation practice, of course, and some Eastern religions have practiced their forms of meditation for more than a thousand years before the advent of Christianity. Don't let this put you off. As a follower of Jesus Christ, your Quiet Prayer practice centers your focus solidly on Jesus Christ, the Lover of your soul.

Don't be confused. Know who you are and know who calls you and desires a deep and intimate relationship with you. Say His name: Jesus Christ.

The Sermon on the Mount

HERE IS A FAMOUS PORTION OF SCRIPTURE FOR US to contemplate. The three Persons of the Godhead are vitally alive in our lives. In Quiet Prayer it's critical to recognize that it's the Holy Spirit bringing us into the presence of God. Because God is invisible and His Spirit is invisible within us, it's impossible for our finite selves to comprehend what's invisible. The finite can never figure out the infinite God, although humans have been trying to do it for eons. Because He's Spirit He can only be known by spirit.

Hundreds of other forms of meditation do just fine focusing on things they can see, feel, touch, and imagine. Not so for us. The only way we can focus on the invisible Father God is to focus from within. We connect with the Holy Spirit because the Holy Spirit within us unites us to God mysteriously and supernaturally. We see God with our spiritual eyes, not our natural eyes.

Let's carry ourselves over to Matthew 5:3–12, to Jesus' Sermon on the Mount and look at it from the holy lens of His Spirit. Here is how the New King James Version reads:

> Blessed are the poor in spirit,
> For theirs is the kingdom of heaven.
> Blessed are those who mourn,
> For they shall be comforted.
> Blessed are the meek,
> For they shall inherit the earth.

Blessed are those who hunger and thirst for
   righteousness,
For they shall be filled.
Blessed are the merciful,
For they shall obtain mercy.
Blessed are the pure in heart,
For they shall see God.
Blessed are the peacemakers,
For they shall be called sons of God.
Blessed are those who are persecuted for righteousness'
   sake,
For theirs is the kingdom of heaven.

Blessed are you when they revile and persecute you, and
say all kinds of evil against you falsely for My sake. Rejoice and
be exceedingly glad, for great is your reward in heaven, for so
they persecuted the prophets who were before you.

Here's a short introduction about this great event in biblical
history. When Jesus came to earth as man, He not only brought
blessing to the world, He was Blessing. He continues to be supernatural Blessing through infinity. One day, full of the Holy Spirit's
anointing, He observed the crowds of people waiting for Him and
positioned Himself on the side of a mountain so everyone could
hear Him. He sat down to preach, as was befitting of a revered
rabbi. He preached this message not only for the multitudes surrounding Him on that mountain, but for countless millions of
souls throughout all generations.

To understand the Sermon on the Mount, it is important to first see that Jesus is supernatural blessing, glory, power, joy, beauty, strength, and wisdom to the world. He lived on earth as all man and all God. As all God, He is all Holy Spirit. As all Holy Spirit and all human at the same time, He early on made the conscious choice to be One in Spirit with God. He overcame the lower human self, proving Himself the living reality of God on earth. "If you've seen Me you've seen the Father."

Filled with God by His Holy Spirit, Jesus performed miracles, healed the sick, raised the dead, and tirelessly taught the nature, heart, and love of God. "I can do nothing of my own will but only that which the Father—" As He lived solely by the power of the Holy Spirit of God, so can we. We'll never be sinless as He was, of course, but when He willingly handed over His human life to die in agony on the cross, He bequeathed His Spirit to us. As Christians the same Spirit that raised Him from the dead dwells in us (Romans 8:11).

Here's where the blessing comes in and where we can gain a deeper reverence for Quiet Prayer Christian meditation. We can live supernaturally empowered lives infused with blessing (Jesus Himself in the form of the Holy Spirit in us) through all circumstances.

Jesus is the One in whom all the families of the earth are to be blessed (Genesis 12:3). He came not only as our Blessing but to pour out and pronounce blessings on us. We're created as spiritual beings to inherit spiritual blessings.

Each of the Beatitudes is earthshaking. Unexpected. Unreasonable. Without the Holy Spirit impossible. The sermon threw the Pharisees and scribes into an absolute rage. They expected Jesus to give a message on the virtues of good people, people who followed the laws of Moses, religious people. Instead He dove right into who God is in the poor, the weak, the persecuted. Jewish Jesus preached that it was possible to be blessed by God outside of the Mosaic Law. This was blasphemy! And how dare this mere man dole out promises of the kingdom of heaven and of God? They were mortified.

For the religious hierarchy, Jesus' words in this sermon hit like a bomb. He spoke with such authority that immediately they saw Him as dangerous. He was obviously riling up the lower classes, influencing people with the crass and base characteristics of the poor, weak, meek, and sad, and never once mentioning and bestowing the honor owed to the religious leaders who followed the laws of Moses.

The Sermon on the Mount speaks of spiritual blessing, which is the power to overcome, to rise up with joy in spite of circumstances, and which only God can produce in us. The Pharisees couldn't begin to comprehend that Jesus' sermon subtly exalted what the power of the Holy Spirit would accomplish in the lives of all those who believed in Him.

The Beatitudes aren't merely encouraging words to remember that things will get better when they go bad. It's quite possible to go through bad times without God's blessing, and many men have suffered and died terrible deaths cursing God. I've prayed for people on their death beds—despairing, frightened people with no previous knowledge of Jesus—and once they surrendered to Him and His love, a miraculous blessing seemed to come over them.

WE'RE CREATED

AS SPIRITUAL

BEINGS TO

INHERIT

SPIRITUAL

BLESSINGS.

One man exclaimed, a few minutes before he died, "I'm so happy!" His daughter said only God could bring words like that out of his mouth. The blessing Jesus speaks of in the Beatitudes is Himself. The Holy Spirit empowers us and therefore we're blessed even during our last minutes on earth.

Let's look at the Beatitudes through the holy lens of God's Spirit. In Hebrew there's no verb at the beginning of each beatitude so here is how they might read:

BEATITUDE 1: O the bliss of the one who realizes his or her utter helplessness and poverty of spirit, for this one will surrender all for the love of God. This powerful union with God by His Spirit makes him a citizen of the kingdom of heaven. (Think of the "kingdom of heaven" here as Jesus prayed in the Lord's Prayer: "Thy kingdom come . . . on earth as it is in heaven" [RSV], which is God's miraculous presence in us here on earth.)

BEATITUDE 2: O the bliss of the one whose heart is broken, for out of his [or her] sorrow the Holy Spirit of God will embrace and comfort, and they will know the supernatural joy of the Lord.

BEATITUDE 3: O the bliss of the one who has the humility to know his own weaknesses and need for the Holy Spirit's power in his [or her] life. This one put aside ego and selfish desires. The world with its pride will no longer possess him, but he shall possess the world.

BEATITUDE 4: O the bliss of the one who hungers and thirsts for the whole of righteousness, for total immersion in God's will and oneness with Him. This one will be filled with the Holy Spirit and never hunger or thirst again.

BEATITUDE 5: O the bliss of the merciful person because mercy is the very heart of God. The Holy Spirit enables this person to see into the hearts of others and feel with compassion what they feel. Their acts of mercy are one with His.

BEATITUDE 6: (I spin with ecstasy contemplating the sixth beatitude.) O the bliss of the man or woman whose motives are unpolluted like pure metal with no hint of alloy. This person pays the price to love God fully on His terms and completely submits to His Spirit with clear, open, spiritual eyes, the very eyes that see the face of God.

BEATITUDE 7: O the bliss of the one led by the Holy Spirit who not only stands for peace, but does all he or she can to produce peaceful, right relationships between fellow humans, for this one will always be known as a true child of God.

BEATITUDES 8 AND 9: O the bliss of the faithful believer who suffers and is persecuted for Christ, the abused and tortured one for the sake of Christ. It is by the Holy Spirit this one prevails and overcomes torment and death, as the prophets of the past. These are the ones who possess and reign in the kingdom of heaven and, even while alive, enter the glory halls of gladness and joy.

Jesus encouraged those who are slandered and persecuted for His sake to "rejoice and be glad." Imagine. The word *glad* is translated from the Greek verb *agaliasthai*, which means "to leap exceedingly," clearly not possible without the supernatural embodiment of the Holy Spirit. "The joy of the LORD is your strength" (Nehemiah 8:10), and it's only by His joy and the joy of all heaven's heaven that these verses make sense.

Here's where our daily Quiet Prayer meditation practice can bring us to see God in our present state and experience heaven on earth. Quiet Prayer can be the actual experience of heaven on earth because nowhere can you be as close to God as when alone with Him in silence and stillness with the eyes of your heart focused solely on Him. To see Him face to face, no longer through a glass darkly (1 Corinthians 13:12), is to see Him spiritually as yours. He is yours and you are His.

Luke 6:20–49 also records the Sermon on the Mount, and it includes Jesus' naming four types of people who give no thought for God and the Holy Spirit can't reach them (verses 24–26).

1. People who live for money and lavishly spend it on themselves and for pleasure. Jesus says they have their reward.
2. People who live comfortably, eating and getting fat while people around them are hungry. These people are starving without the Holy Spirit.
3. Those who laugh off serious matters concerning the welfare of others and the community. They laugh off their responsibility to be helpful and especially caring. Jesus says their laughter will turn to tears.
4. People who love false flattery and don't care if it's deadly.

Each of these types are victims of their own choosing. They represent the Lower Self without God. You can't get much lower.

Through your Quiet Prayer practice and daily contemplation of His Word, you will enjoy Him as never before, and by the power of His Spirit, you will become more and more like Him. This is happiness. You're satisfied with your likeness to God (Psalm 17:15) and you enjoy your meditation time. You'll see Him forever, and never lose sight of Him. This is heaven's happiness and the joy of the Lord.

Jesus on Earth

JESUS ARRIVED ON EARTH AS A MAN TO SHOW US our true identity, created in His image, and to teach us who the Father is. Quiet Prayer helps bring us to the reality of who we are, who we were born to be, and who God is in us. We come to the reality that in Him our inner beings, the who of who we are, becomes complete. We are complete in Christ.

Though we may know intellectually that Jesus can fulfill our longings, and we're aware of what the Bible says about God's grace and His wondrous supply of blessings to give us an abundant life, our faith can teeter in hard times. I've seen staunch believers turn to the Devil in hard times, and by this I mean they give more attention to the Devil than to God in the situation. They devote more time fighting devils and demons, and talking about devils and demons, than extolling the power and eternal majesty of our God.

They become agitated and aroused with heated emotion instead of resting in God's Word and in who God is. If we're reduced to long episodes of Devil bashing, it's time to take a step back and embrace a holy hush. "Be still, and know that I am God" (Psalm 46:10) is a constant word for us. Don't ignore His still, small voice calling you to fix your attention on loving and trusting God. It doesn't take a spiritual giant to recognize evil in the world, but it takes a child of God to see God.

YOUR QUIET PRAYER
PRACTICE IS AN ACT OF
SUBMITTING. YOU'RE
SUBMITTING TO SILENCE
AND TO GIVING ALL
YOUR ATTENTION TO
THE LORD JESUS.

"Submit to God. Resist the devil and he will flee from you." James 4:7 is an admonition for us all. If we turn it around it reads, "Resist the devil and he will flee from you. Submit to God." Submitting to God is the key. Give God more attention than evil.

Your Quiet Prayer practice is an act of submitting. You're submitting to silence and to giving all your attention to the Lord Jesus. When He walked the earth, Jesus set His focus on God, completely submitted to Him. ("Not My will, but Yours" [Luke 22:42], He prayed to the Father before His crucifixion. That's being submitted to God.)

From His oneness with the Father during His life, He taught us how to break down the barriers inside us by completely submitting to His Holy Spirit's transforming power. How else can we blithely bless our enemies and those who curse and persecute us? We'd have to be drugged to hand over our coats, ask for more when someone slaps us on the face, and walk the extra mile when we have urgent things to do.

The transforming process of the Holy Spirit in us makes it easy to hear what Jesus is saying in Luke 6:27–31, and it's no longer an outrageous thought. We don't get there by forcing ourselves to be nice or by wishing we could turn the cheek, give the coat, walk the mile; it's by dedicated spiritual work.

The work isn't about mastering the difficult deeds in this chapter, it's about being submitted to God, which is the work of Quiet Prayer. In Quiet Prayer your focus is on God Himself, not on doing anything. As your spirit enlarges and blossoms more and more in His Spirit, you discover that what once was an outrageous idea is now reasonable.

IN QUIET PRAYER

YOUR FOCUS IS

ON GOD HIMSELF,

NOT ON DOING

ANYTHING.

But I say to you who hear: Love your enemies, do good to those who hate you, bless those who curse you, and pray for those who spitefully use you. To him who strikes you on the one cheek, offer the other also. And from him who takes away your cloak, do not withhold your tunic either. Give to everyone who asks of you. And from him who takes away your goods do not ask them back. And just as you want men to do to you, you also do to them likewise.

As a Christian it would be good to read Luke 6:27–36 at least once a week.

Mysterious Ways

ON THE DAY GOD SET OUT TO CREATE HUMAN beings, He sculpted an exquisite composite of bones, tissue, muscle, cells, and atoms, and then designed a brain and each of the body's major functions, heart, liver, lungs, kidneys, and need I go on? Let's just summarize by saying He created us body, soul, and spirit, which is amazing in itself to contemplate. David did just that when he marveled at how wonderfully he was "knit together" in his mother's womb.

> I will praise You, for I am fearfully and wonderfully
>   made;
> Marvelous are Your works,
> And that my soul knows very well.
>
> (PSALM 139:14)

Notice David said, "My soul knows very well." In other words, he knew with his mind. He recognized and marveled at his creation intellectually.

> For thus says the high and lofty One—
> He Who inhabits eternity, Whose name is Holy:
> I dwell in the high and holy place.
>
> (ISAIAH 57:15 AMPC)

The verse goes on to remind us that we will never be able to fully figure out why He does and does not do certain things. He is not a person to be analyzed. He is God of all creation.

But God did something else that opens wide the mystery and the glorious wonder of our creation. Ecclesiastes 3:11 tells us God created human beings with eternity in our hearts. Eternity lies inside us.

> *He has made everything beautiful in its time.* He also has planted eternity in men's hearts and minds [a divinely implanted sense of a purpose working through the ages which nothing under the sun but God alone can satisfy]. (AMPC, emphasis added)

He inhabits eternity, and eternity lives in our hearts. When is the last time you contemplated the God-kissed fact that inside you, deep inside you, in your heart and mind dwells all of eternity?

The most common interpretation of eternity is that it's something never-ending, timeless, or infinite. Now think of eternity as a place. A particular place. Eternity is the place God inhabits. Jesus said, "I go to prepare a place for you" (John 14:2). That place is in you now. That's eternity itself.

We have everything built in us to know God and lead lives intimately connected with Him. Our bodies house our souls, which are comprised of our intellect, emotions, and will, and our spirits are the vehicles for God's Spirit to fill with Himself. We have everything we need inside us (His Holy Spirit) to keep us in close harmony with God.

The next thing to do is to bring eternity from our hearts

(our minds) into our spirits. As a Christian your spirit is already enlivened by the Holy Spirit, and eternity dwells inside you. This happened when you gave your life to Jesus Christ. You are someone who will live forever, and eternity dwells inside you. That's a mystery so great you have to live it to know it.

Early Parents

They're not exactly Mummy and Daddy, but we know we're related. They were God's first human creation and I'm talking, of course, about Adam and Eve. Think for a minute about Adam and Eve, our parents who were cast out of Eden. They were created with eternity in their hearts, like us, but they overrode their hearts and exercised their natural will to make a choice. They chose to bite into the fruit of the knowledge of good and evil.

They were never meant to know about evil with its ugliness, sin, and misery, and as a result, they were no longer fit to live in the perfect, sinless Eden. They were now infected with the knowledge of hatred, tragedy, and suffering. Their happy life in blissful Eden was finished, and they were banished to a world they chose with the knowledge of evil tucked into their damaged souls.

But here's where the compassionate heart of the Lord comes in. Adam and Eve may have been banished from Eden, but they weren't banished from God. They left with eternity still in their hearts. They weren't alone, nor were they separated from divine purpose. God banished them from the perfect dwelling of Eden, but not from Himself.

We, like Adam and Eve, are created spirit, soul, and body in the image of God. He planted eternity in our hearts. This is incredibly humbling. Knowing God, really knowing Him, is extremely humbling. The humble self is our true, Higher Self who is without guile, who is selfless and at peace with God's will.

God works "in mysterious ways" and always those mysterious ways are connected to His Holy Spirit. Quiet Prayer invisibly enlarges our human spirits with His to be centered within His inviting presence in Christ Jesus. In silence and without words He teaches us to know His presence in an altogether transforming way. Eternity can miraculously nudge us in our daily thoughts, actions, behavior, and choices.

God and *Your* Eternity

Before you sit for your second Quiet Prayer time, consider this:

In Quiet Prayer you consciously choose to sit in silence with the God of all eternity. Eternity dwells within your heart (your mind).

As you choose to focus on the living, eternal God, you naturally enter the living presence of eternity.

Becoming more aware that eternity is alive in you and that eternity also surrounds you by the Holy Spirit, you experience a shift in the choices you make.

Resting in the royal halls of eternity every day in Quiet Prayer helps you to be more alive and aware of who you are, and who God created you to be. Quiet Prayer brings you to your higher self where you enjoy being you.

Sharing Eternity with Angels

God's angels live and thrive in God's eternity. One of the most electrifying statements spoken by an angel is when the angel Gabriel appeared to the priest Zacharias as he prayed in the temple (Luke 1:11). The angel Gabriel announced great news to the priest, explaining that he and his wife, Elizabeth, would give birth to a son even though they were both way too old to bear children. The violent protests of Zacharias didn't shake up Gabriel. He looked at Zacharias and said these words, "I stand in the presence of God."

What a mind-blowing statement. Here was a major angelic being standing in front of Zacharias, an angel whose entire existence throughout eternity is spent in the face-to-face presence of God. We can take his words to mean that Zacharias is in big trouble for arguing with an angel or that Gabriel is making the proclamation that he, God's holy angel, lives in, thrives in, knows, and eternally chooses to stand in the presence of perfect love. Gabriel knows God.

How do you suppose the angel Gabriel and the angelic host know God? By telling Him their problems? By continually asking for things and calling it prayer? By complaining about the sad state of the world? By flattering Him, blessing their food before dinner? How is it angels know Him so well? The angels know God by standing in His presence.

Precisely what we do in Quiet Prayer meditation.

THE ANGELS

KNOW GOD

BY STANDING

IN HIS

PRESENCE.

Agape with New Eyes

KNOWING GOD'S LOVE GOES FAR DEEPER THAN OUR experiences. God will shower you with countless blessings every day. But too often, without realizing it, we tend to know Him only by what He does for us. Without knowing Him as Love, we're unprepared for life's terrible ups and downs. With very little spiritual experience of His character and mind outside answered prayers and blessings, we can be horribly disappointed, crushed, and even bitter when bad things happen.

God is not knowable through our minds alone. We can't think Him into reality. The reason is, He is Spirit and can only be known in the spirit. He is Love and because He is Spirit, we can be transformed by His love. Inside the power of His love, He is entirely knowable.

God, as Himself, is not knowable through our intellects, no matter how brilliant. We can know about God, but not really know Him. For example, we know He created all there is and we know He is all powerful. True. That's somewhat like saying, "I know Andy because he's from Minneapolis and rides a Harley." I don't really know Andy at all, do I? In order to know Andy, I'd have to know who he is inside; otherwise I'm just looking at his physical description. With God, we look inside at His love, and there we find Him waiting.

What if Andy did nice things for me? What if I called him up and asked him to shovel the walk and he'd do it? What if he also made a run to the post office for me? What if I needed my computer fixed, my website updated, and Andy was right on it? Sounds like an employee, doesn't it? Love doesn't treat God like an employee.

Agape perfectly characterizes the love Jesus has for His Father and for you and me. God is agape love. Yet He's beyond agape. The Greek word *agápē* is defined in two ways: the first is "the perfect, flawless eternal love of God." The second is active on our parts. It refers to our human selfless, sacrificial, unconditional love for others.

The source of all love is God. Love is God, perfect and eternal. He is Love (capital *L*). The human emotion of love is fine, but when that love is spiritually charged by the source of Love, it's beyond agape.

Going beyond agape love is to take the holy leap into God Himself and forget ourselves. This is exactly what happens in Quiet Prayer. We bring all of ourselves, who we are inside and out, to God. No pretenses, no excuses, no hesitancies, guilt, shyness, fear, or doubt. We leave our needs and requests aside. We choose Him for Himself, not for answers to our prayers. No words.

We bring everything we are to Him and He envelops us, needs and all, in Himself. We don't need words. Perfect love meets us exactly as we are in that very moment of time. This is pure agape love. You lovingly surrender all of you to all of God in the silence. This experience of your spirit swollen wide with the living presence of God by His Holy Spirit is agape love. This is the meaning of holy communion: one with Christ in you.

WE CHOOSE HIM

FOR HIMSELF, NOT

FOR ANSWERS

TO OUR PRAYERS.

NO WORDS.

Only now does agape love make sense. All the good things you do for others is the outpouring of what takes place in Quiet Prayer when you and the love of God are united as one. In your daily life, you and God do good together. It's not you doing the work with Him somewhere up in the ethos watching you. His blessing and anointing are in you; you are in Him, and all you do in His name you do together as one. Your job is to show up. Jesus does the work.

Is God Beyond Agape?

WE CAN ONLY KNOW GOD, THE CREATOR OF ALL there is, by knowing Him in His love. I'm talking about a deeper level than outer experiences. Expect the blessings and the hand of God in every area of your life because God will shower you with countless blessings every day. But too often without knowing Him as Love, we're clueless. We have very little of the awareness of Him that He wants to reveal to us.

God is not knowable through our minds alone. (I'll repeat this a lot.) Inside the power of His love, however, He is entirely knowable.

My evangelist friend tells me she's always in the presence of God. She doesn't need Quiet Prayer to get in the presence of God. When she's ministering to others the presence of God is very heavy on her. She can feel it in her entire being. When she's on her knees praying for others, the presence of God can overwhelm her to tears. I completely understand. I want to shout hallelujah. Yes! Be overwhelmed.

"Me too," I tell her.

There are many kinds of prayer, as I'm always repeating, and many ways to celebrate our love for Him. If they honor the Lord, why not love them all?

You'll find that all your communication with the Lord is enhanced by the moments you spend alone with Him in Quiet Prayer. Your intense moments of intercession for others will be reinforced with deeper vision and confidence if you begin your prayer session with Quiet Prayer. Meet with the Lord in silence before asking for needs to be met—and even before praise and worship. Notice how your attitude and use of language changes.

Your periods of Bible study and contemplation of God's Word are enriched because you're accustomed to being alone in the presence of the Lord, so it's only natural that you will understand His Word with clearer insight. It is especially true the other way around. Your study of God's Word illuminates your understanding and adoration of who God is.

Quiet Prayer has brought my own regular prayer life to a far higher relational place. In praying for myself, the world, or the specific needs of others, I'm aware that I'm praying as a soul who is one with Jesus and that the Holy Spirit is at the core of me. His concerns are my concerns. At times I spend more time thanking Him than sending up my list of petitions because I remember what He has said about Himself in His Word and what He has taught me through silence in His presence. I team up with eternity inside my heart and I pray without borders. There could be no more sublime privilege.

We don't have to be evangelists or ministers to feel the incomparable presence of God on us and around us. When I'm on the platform teaching or preaching, I can feel the presence of God, but I can also feel the presence of God when I'm puttering around the house or walking the dog. The presence of God is most powerful when in intercessory prayer. Being alert to His presence is absolutely necessary.

I've spoken in churches when the presence of God has been

so intense I thought I was in heaven. I've also had the experience of being on the phone with a Christian sister and the presence of God is so strong we couldn't talk (a miracle).

We don't always feel the presence of God in outward ways, but we can increase those experiences by being spiritually aware. He is always with us ("Lo, I am with you always."), but too often we aren't aware of it. We wait for special times to think about His presence.

More on "feelings" in a later chapter.

YOU'LL FIND THAT ALL

YOUR COMMUNICATION

WITH THE LORD IS

ENHANCED BY THE

MOMENTS YOU SPEND

ALONE WITH HIM IN

QUIET PRAYER.

When the Holy Spirit
Wasn't Quiet

In the spectacular second chapter of Acts, we read how the Holy Spirit fell on the expectant believers at Pentecost. I should say He exploded on them. They were waiting in the Upper Room as Jesus had instructed, and suddenly, "like a mighty, rushing wind" (more like a holy tsunami), the presence of God by His Spirit dropped down and into them.

That outpouring changed the world forever. It was a crucial pivotal point in human history. The very same Spirit that raised Christ from the dead (Romans 8:11) would now dwell inside each of us. At Pentecost the Holy Spirit not only fell upon the believers, He entered their hearts, which is how they could speak in other tongues, perform miracles, and preach with supernatural anointing.

Here's where Quiet Prayer comes in. Alone, in silence with the living power of Pentecost, with the Creator of all there is, with the Lover of our souls, we do absolutely nothing but remain in His presence inside us and surrounding us. We're at attention, concentrating on Him, quiet, wordless, and shrouded in mutual love.

Here's the key: when we feel the presence of God surrounding us and upon us, we sense and feel amazing love. In Quiet Prayer it's our love pouring out of us to Him. It's as though we're falling upon Him with our presence and our love. We're locked as one, and it's all in silence. Quiet Prayer, Christian meditation, is a completely spiritual event. We're not speaking, we're not praising Him, singing, dancing, or expressing our love physically except by being still and focused on Him. Our facial muscles are relaxed. There's no tension in our bodies. We are one with God in the Spirit.

Can we really be alone with God in the Spirit and not be meditating? Of course! Meditation is in addition to our daily walk and prayer life with God. It's different and more intense, though. I'll say it again: Quiet Prayer doesn't replace other forms of prayer. It doesn't replace the wonderful experience of feeling God's presence at other times. Quiet Prayer adds to these experiences.

Be alert. Be ready.

Imagine if those waiting in the Upper Room at Pentecost noted a mighty wind heading their way and ran for cover. Imagine them cowering and shivering under the staircase until it was over. No, they were alert and waiting for the promise Jesus made them, and God gave them who they were waiting for: His Holy Spirit.

More About Our Ancestors

WE HAVE A WONDERFUL HERITAGE. CHRISTIANITY in the twelfth and thirteenth centuries became marked with intellectualism and anti-rationalism. Debate peppered the church at large. Those who pursued the spiritual life of meditation—contemplation centered on the love of God through Jesus—weren't always monks or clerics. These deeply spiritual Christian heroes and heroines were called mystics. Among these holy men and women emerged a woman called Hadewijch of Antwerp.

Hadewijch of Antwerp

A vibrant, contemplative woman of the first half of the thirteenth century, Hadewijch was an influence in the lives of several leaders of the church, including Meister Ekhart. It wasn't until the end of the nineteenth century that a manuscript of Hadewijch's written in Flemish was discovered at the Royal Library of Brussels. It was around the end of World War I that specialists and scholars confirmed, through her many letters and poems, that Hadewijch's compositions were "not only the work of unrivalled linguistic and literary interest, but the testimony of a very great mystic."[1]

The Inquisition was raging across Europe and Spain at this time, and corruption in the Catholic Church was rampant. So-called heretics, or non-Catholics, were tortured, murdered, and burned at the stake by the tens of thousands. Hadewijch was part of a lay religious order formed outside ecclesiastical authority and therefore condemned. Many of these women chose to live the gospel to its depths in the manner of the early abbas and ammas of the desert. Hadewijch taught that once we experience the true divine love of God, we will never know anything to exceed it.

Hadewijch was a visionary as was Joan of Arc, her contemporary. Spiritual gifts such as experiencing heavenly visions, effecting miracles in Jesus' name, or any appearance of the gifts of the Holy Spirit were considered heresy. Hadewijch and her disciples existed apart from society as laypeople dedicated to the Father's love in Christ. In fact, God's love was the single theme of Hadewijch's ministry.

> . . . the theme of an incomparable love, of a love that belongs only to God. For that is the only love that gives all, that gives itself, that is only pure gift.

In a medieval world of the Inquisition strangled with inhuman suffering and madness, a world where evil was so vile and bloody no human being was safe from its religious claws, this little woman preached on God's love. Hadewijch herself often had to flee for her life. She referred to herself as a wanderer.

> To love Him [God] is to love all that He loves, as He Himself, and He alone can love.

Hadewijch and the desert ammas and abbas, and every saint, mystic, and anointed martyr through the ages possessed two things in common: fearlessness and meditation.

Fearlessness. As the apostle Paul wrote, "For me to live is Christ; to die is gain," these early men and women of faith didn't think twice about their own lives. Their life companion was the love of God, nothing else. Their lives embodied the words "Perfect love casts out fear."

Meditation. Yes, meditation. Again and again the early mothers and fathers of faith spoke of their hours alone with God. Hours and hours in solitude with Jesus, bathing in His presence.

Pure unity with God is not possible with our human intellect or with much talk and reasoning. To know Jesus, to unite our love with Love Himself, demands a training in solitude. It demands we regularly withdraw from our daily routine for a period of silence with Him. It's in silence you learn to see God for who He is. Here is one of Hadewijch's many poems.

Love's Constancy

Anyone who has waded

Through Love's turbulent waters,

Now feeling hunger and now satiety,

Is untouched by the season

Of withering or blooming,

QUIET PRAYER

For in the deepest and most dangerous waters,

On the highest peaks,

Love is always the same[2]

Going Deeper

GOD FITS HIS HOLY SPIRIT INTO YOUR SPIRIT. HE measures your capacity for His divine presence to fit comfortably into your openness to Him. Paul wrote to the Corinthian Christians that he fed them with spiritual milk because they couldn't handle spiritual meat. It was not only an admonishment to go deeper in the Lord, it was also considerate. He knew that it required more than a slightly developed spirit to grasp the greatness of the spiritual riches he wanted to share. Jesus told his disciples, "I have many things to say to you, but you cannot bear them now" (John 16:12). The lesson for us is to go deeper. "Be filled with the Holy Spirit" (Ephesians 5:18). Filled. Not partially, not content with spiritual nibbles but *filled*. Paul wrote to the Colossians, "We do not cease to pray for you, and to desire that you might be *filled* with the knowledge of his [God's] will in all wisdom and spiritual understanding."

Jesus won't withhold Himself when invited. Widen your mind and heart for Jesus and His presence, and He meets you right where you are spiritually. He calls you now to open your spirit to His. He wants a deeper relationship with you, just as you need a deeper relationship with Him.

I believe we all hunger for a deeper relationship with God. The barriers that hold us back originate in our Lower Self. Through Quiet Prayer we put an end to these negative roadblocks to deeper spiritual lives. We learn to recognize how we can be controlled by the perceptions and dictates of our egos. Did you know your Christian life can be ego driven? Your surrender to daily Quiet Prayer helps to squash the power of your ego to make room for spiritual transformation to take place.

The transformation we long for is not for the purpose of doing something or getting better at something, or even achieving spiritual tasks. If you're in ministry, it's especially important you maintain a Quiet Prayer practice because it's vital to quiet yourself and concentrate on God in silent meditation. This form of total surrender is imperative. Your needs and your ministry's needs can easily consume your prayer life, which is exhausting. The transformation you need from God in order to clearly hear from God will only bring brighter life to your work.

Quiet Prayer is an intimate union and commitment with God. If we receive direction, anointing for ministry, power for great deeds, that's wonderful. Because of your time spent in Quiet Prayer, you'll discover that your will becomes more solidly aligned with His will and great things take place, greater than you even asked for.

But as it is written:

> "Eye has not seen, nor ear heard,
> Nor have entered into the heart of man
> The things which God has prepared for those who love
> Him."

(1 CORINTHIANS 2:9)

QUIET PRAYER

IS AN INTIMATE

UNION AND

COMMITMENT

WITH GOD.

The key word in this verse is *love*. First John 4:19 explains how love overtakes us: We love Him because He loved us first. Our love for Him grows within us as we learn to know Him more intimately. Listen to this from my favorite psalm:

> Because he has set his love upon Me, therefore I will
>   deliver him;
> I will set him on high, because he has known My
>   name.
> He shall call upon Me, and I will answer him.
>
> (PSALM 91:14–15)

Notice how the Holy Spirit confirms a truth again and again throughout the Bible.

The daily practice of Quiet Prayer is an act of love. You can't help it.

If you come to meditation to earn something from God or to win His favor, you miss the point because you already possess His favor, and within you is everything you need. You're locked in His love and He wants only the best for you. Now just sit with Him and be quiet.

QUIET PRAYER PRACTICE #2

THIS IS YOUR SECOND QUIET PRAYER PRACTICE IN this book. As you get ready, think about how you'll enjoy this time with God. Meditation, sitting alone in silence with God, is a gift to enjoy. Unlike secular meditation, Quiet Prayer is a process of concentrating on God. We lose our concentration and we come back. We lose our concentration and we come back again. It's the coming back to our focus of concentration— God—that transforms.

1. Seek out a quiet place. Sit in a comfortable, upright, alert position with spine straight, shoulders back, head relaxed, and your eyes lightly closed.

2. Quiet your body. This might take a minute or two while you still your mind and settle into your body. Breathe deeply and slowly with nice, even breaths in and out.

3. Quietly begin to speak to yourself the sacred word or phrase you select. Listen to it as it gently rests in your mind.

4. Set your timer and gently sound your bell.

5. Close your eyes.

6. Focus your attention on God who is in you and with you. Jesus greets our spirits, and for the next moments the world falls away from you and you are one with God.

7. Remain still and focused. When thoughts race through

your mind, gently brush them aside with your sacred
word.

8. At the closing sound of your timer, pause, breathe, and
gently open your eyes.

9. Sound your bell three times. One to take a beautiful
breath to breathe in what you've just experienced; one
to come back to your daily life; and one to be grateful.

10. Remain still for a moment to take note of the various
thoughts that may have risen as you sat in meditation. Is
there a pattern to these thoughts? Are they daydreams
of grandeur? Are they laced with fear? Are they of the
past? Future planning? Recognize and name them. You
may want to jot down your observations.

TIP: I have found that when I begin my Quiet Prayer session and I tell the Lord something along the lines of, "This is my
time with You, Lord. Just You and me alone," that I'm able to
focus on Jesus more quickly. This may help you too. I confess
that I'm not totally at the wordless point of Quiet Prayer practice
yet. And that's all right. There's no judgment in Quiet Prayer. No
rights and wrongs. No demands. No iron-clad rules.

Remember

In this place for these minutes:

    You haven't a care in the world.

    You have nowhere to go, nothing to do.

    You haven't a single responsibility,

        not a single duty to perform.

In this place for these minutes:

    All that exists is you and God.

    Nothing else.

    There's nobody to please,

        no pressures to do anything at all.

    No past, no future,

        only here in this space with God

        right now.

The best of all is, when the Lord visits us and never goes away but stays with us always, so that we walk in the light of His countenance and go from strength to strength, always, Thy visitation never ended, daily continued, preserves my spirit.

—C. H. Spurgeon

Living Right Now

You're here right now.
Holding this book.
Breathing this air.
There's only now.
The past is done.
The future is itself.
For better or worse,
Right now
Is all you have.

LOOK AT YOURSELF WITH YOUR SPIRITUAL EYES AND see that the Spirit of God is fused into your human spirit right now. At this moment.

The Bible says you have the mind of Christ *now*. Present tense.

"We have the mind of Christ" (1 Corinthians 2:16).

The Bible also says that when you're confused and when you're dealing with horrific life issues, you must not act out: "Not by might [your own or an entire army's], nor by power [your own or a whole nation's], but by My Spirit" (Zechariah 4:6). How can this scripture make sense to you if you think God is running late somewhere out in the vast unknown future? Or if He's tied up in some past? His Spirit lives in you now.

God is in you now.

The foundation for thriving in Quiet Prayer, as well as in our lives, is the known presence of the Holy Spirit within us. Our consent to the Holy Spirit's invitation to empowerment is key to everything in our lives. Just as you can "rejoice and be glad" in impossible suffering, so can you rise up in your Higher Self empowered to overcome stress, worry, fear, and anger.

We thrive in Quiet Prayer because the Holy Spirit is our foundation and because it's He who crowns us with discipline, the stick-to-itiveness, and the enjoyment of our daily sits.

Do you see how daily Quiet Prayer practice cannot help but lift us to a higher place in God, a place where we find home? We aren't visitors in the "secret place of the Most High," our home, we're permanent residents. We're permanently fixed.

Of the countless forms of meditation I've examined, I have to conclude that without the Holy Spirit of God through Jesus Christ, the positive results achieved are missing eternity. Other forms may help people arrive at certain levels of serenity, but the serenity, no matter how wonderfully attained, will die with the person. The Holy Spirit is infinite. With our spirits open to and filled with no other spirit but the Holy Spirit, we're operating with eternity in us even if we're absolute newbies at this business of meditation. I always say if you're seriously flawed, all the better. Come join the rest of us flawed souls and learn Quiet Prayer.

In Quiet Prayer there's no judgment. We're all pilgrims.

This book is an invitation for each of us to know the Holy Spirit in more depth.

IN QUIET

PRAYER

THERE'S NO

JUDGMENT.

WE'RE ALL

PILGRIMS.

To Be

LET'S LOOK AT ANOTHER ASPECT OF QUIET PRAYER: the aspect of *being*. Lest I sound like a New Age guru from a woodsy ashram somewhere up north, let me preface this with Scripture. The first word in Psalm 46:10 is *be*. Ponder this: The sacred presence of God is all you possess. Be in *be*ing with all of you. God is hidden in plain sight. Your only job in Quiet Prayer is to keep still and be.

Be still, and know that I am God. (Psalm 46:10)

The two great events of your life are first, when you're born, and second, when you find out why.

Your Brain

Hardwired Negative

Neuroscience research tells us that we are hardwired to register and remember negative events more quickly and deeply than positive ones.

A happy brain is shaped differently than an unhappy one, but neuroscience and the Bible tell us that through training exercises an unhappy brain can be molded to actually look like a happy one. Neuropsychologists explain the concept of neuroplasticity, specifically how the brain's physical shape can be changed. The shape of the brain can be changed under the influence of external events.

Your brain is hardwired to latch on to unhappy and upsetting events, which create an unhappily shaped brain.

How Your Brain Works

Let's look at the biblical account of creation. In the beginning, God designed the human brain for joy, love, trust, and happiness, with no negative neural pathways. But when Adam chose to know evil and was removed from the perfect, sinless garden of Eden, his brain mechanism had to adjust to a different environment, an environment of harm, danger, and pain. Out in the cold, cruel world and no longer blissfully unaware of danger or evil, Adam now had to contend with those things.

His world was no longer perfect. His brain, therefore, had to adjust to anticipate and overcome dangers. Adam's brain became a tool to protect him from pain and to figure out ways to solve problems. The brain became negativity biased. As a result, dangers, pains, and problems are the events that capture our brain's attention to this day. The human nervous system, psychologist Rick Hanson wrote, "scans for, reacts to, stores, and recalls negative information about oneself and one's world. The brain is like Velcro for negative experiences and Teflon for positive ones."[1] The natural result is a growing residue of emotional pain, pessimism, and numbing inhibition in implicit memory.

The brain makes distinctions between two types of memory: implicit and explicit. Explicit memory empowers us to do things like remember the names of our friends or where we parked the car. On the other hand, implicit, or emotional, memories are formed unconsciously. These memories are viscerally, rather than logically, initiated.

The amygdala of the brain, which is an almond-shaped set of neurons deep in the brain's temporal lobe, acts as the switchboard in implicit memory, a response to outside stimuli. It's neurologically primed to label experiences as frightening and threatening. Once the amygdala flags an episode as negative, it immediately stores the event and compares it to the record of other painful experiences. If a pattern match is found, a series of chemical reactions signals alarm. These events occur to protect us from harm, but as a result, the bad things that happen are registered and responded to almost instantaneously, whereas the happy events take five to twenty seconds just to begin to register.

Our daily stress releases glucocorticoids that can kill cells in the hippocampus in the brain. The swirl of chemical reactions due to stress dictates the brain's helpless, persistent focus on negativity. We're killing ourselves with the negative input to our brains.

The good news is, the brain can be retrained. Quiet Prayer helps to deliberately revive our brains. Have you noticed how swiftly nervousness, stress, anger, or fear can overtake you compared to feelings of peace, joy, inner stillness, or genuine happiness? You can turn that around. Leading a genuinely happy life doesn't happen without our deliberate effort, or retraining our brains. Deliberate, conscious effort is a function of the higher regions of the brain.

There are fascinating studies by researchers who took brain scans of people who regularly engaged in some form of meditation and meditative prayer and those with no meditation experience. Researchers found that after an eight-week meditation program not only did the higher regions of the brain thicken, but the amygdala also became less dense in the praying people. They were happier. Now wellness health centers and hospitals offer different forms of meditation to patients for pain management and to protect against stress-related disorders and depression.

We should pray more?

Yes.

The Beautiful Brain Effects of Quiet Prayer

When you enter stillness and focus your attention on God, you are creating new positive neural pathways in your brain.

THE GOOD NEWS IS,

THE BRAIN CAN BE

RETRAINED. QUIET

PRAYER HELPS TO

DELIBERATELY REVIVE

OUR BRAINS.

Think of these new neural pathways as clear, positive avenues for thought. Your intense focus on God, who is all good, forces the negative neural pathways to shrink. They're still there, but because of the brain's plasticity, your Quiet Prayer practice continually works to create new, positive space for your mind to rest.

It's a fact. Science agrees with the Bible. Neuroscientists recognize that human beings who practice prayer and meditation are happier people than those who do not. Prayer, of all things!

Not a better environment, not health, not DNA, not social status, not money, not success, not wealth, but prayerful meditation makes people happier.

There are thousands of different forms and methods for meditation. Christian meditation, or Quiet Prayer, is the process of quieting and resting the mind, which is totally different from our normal, active state of mind. The practice of Quiet Prayer opens our awareness to who we are and elevates us to the center of our beings, which is Christ.

David wrote, "The meditation of my heart shall give understanding" (Psalm 49:3).

The confidence gained in the Word of God, contemplation, and Quiet Prayer bolsters us up in the face of difficulty and stress. We've developed brain habits to steady us. The peace of God has built roadways in our brains to a new way of living and thinking. "I shall not be moved for it is well with my soul" has become our mantra.

The Dominion of the Mind

WHAT KEEPS US FROM KNOWING THAT GOD IS WITH us and in us? It boils down to one thing, and it's not anxiety or doubt or any other emotional state or condition. We have to ask ourselves where these feelings originate, and the only answer is: in our minds.

When we consider our minds and how littered they can be with useless busyness, but at the same time molded with acumen and brilliance, we're faced with a paradox. Though we can't live without our active minds, it's the mind that is our instrument of defeat.

There's that expression of frustration, "I think I'm losing my mind." Where do you suppose your mind runs off to? I can picture myself bounding down the street interrogating bystanders, "Have you seen my mind anywhere? It's the one with all the useless clutter, the one wasted with stupid mind-wandering, daydreaming, and misbeliefs."

When I take the time to quiet my hyperactive mind in Quiet Prayer, I allow my spiritual inner life to take precedence in the moment.

As much as 83 percent of human thought is said to be useless, wasted energy. Our minds go whirling about without control for most of our lives. However, when we're working out a problem; studying; thinking up equations and solutions; memorizing words, maps, or even dance steps, we call that concentrating. Do these acts of concentration enrich our lives? Yes, because they're creating or maintaining the positive neural pathways of the brain.

Negative concentration or obsessing on something grossly unpleasant forms negative neural pathways in the brain that help you tumble into a state of misery quite easily. Over time you're stuck with a lack of forgiveness, anger, faultfinding, mistrust, and even a perceived distance from God.

Quiet Prayer teaches us to let go of obsessions, painful memories, hurts, and injustices. It's not therapy; it's easing back into who we were born to be.

The beauty is, you know God has your agenda on His mind, as well as your work, family, ministry, health, relationships, city, country, and world. You can let go and simply enjoy the brief moments you have alone with Him without a single care. Right now your calendar is empty. We can't think God into our spirits. In your mind you may think you have to change or fix things. You may think you must control things, work things out.

Be at peace right now in the now. Quiet Prayer is the tool to show you to be glad in the presence of God. In your daily life you'll become more aware of the things you think about and in time develop new habits of purposeful focus. By letting go of untamed thoughts in Quiet Prayer, you develop spiritual muscle for your daily life.

"Letting go" has become a culture in itself. You'll hear it in popular psychological circles and wherever people are trying to improve themselves. For us as contemplative Christians, letting go during Quiet Prayer means that we rest in our knowledge of who we are in Christ and who He is in us, and we let go of all else.

The things that once nagged at our peace and jumbled our minds like thoughts of doubt, fear, worry, and anxiety are now slowly evaporating through the diligent work we do in Quiet Prayer.

We simply become better persons. We learn, for instance, how to be interested in people on a genuine level. We learn how to listen!

LETTING GO DURING

QUIET PRAYER MEANS

THAT WE REST IN OUR

KNOWLEDGE OF WHO

WE ARE IN CHRIST AND

WHO HE IS IN US, AND

WE LET GO OF ALL ELSE.

The Power of Listening

OUR UNION WITH JESUS AND HIS LOVE TRANSCENDS words. Our words are insufficient. Jesus used words and action in everyday life, of course, but in times of prayer He withdrew into solitude. Jesus is the Word. God doesn't disapprove of our busy and active lives. He never says in Scripture to stop what we're doing and forget all about work. In fact, the Word of God tells us just the opposite:

> For even when we were with you, we commanded you this: If anyone will not work, neither shall he eat. (2 Thessalonians 3:10)

It's our anxiety He addressed: "Let not your heart be troubled." "Peace I give you, not as the world gives—" (John 14:1, 27, paraphrased).

In the familiar account of Jesus and His disciples having dinner at the home of His friend Lazarus and Lazarus's two sisters, Mary and Martha, a conflict arose. Mary forgot all about dinner and sat mesmerized by what Jesus was talking about. She sat enraptured, listening to His every word while Martha anxiously labored preparing food. Finally she burst into the room where Jesus was teaching and spouted out what amounted to, "Jesus, tell my sister to come help me. Here I am stuck with all the work while she does nothing."

Jesus, in His sweet way, responded with, "Martha, Martha,

you're worried and upset about many things." He told her that Mary had made a good decision when she chose to be still and sit at His feet to learn about God. He told Martha that few things in this life are actually necessary, but there was really only one thing that mattered and what Mary learned could never be taken away from her.

The practical side of me can't help wonder if they ate at all that night. Did Martha take off her apron and sit down to listen too? Did her brother Lazarus get up and stir the soup? Did the bread burn in the oven? Maybe Jesus Himself set the table. Maybe they stayed up all night nibbling on burnt bread and cold soup while Jesus taught.

The words that remain with us like fire are His words to Martha: "Martha, Martha . . ."

It was not her busy activity Jesus addressed, but her anxiety. She was nervous and upset, and Jesus discerned that she was anxious about more than just the dinner. "Many things," He said.

The early believers learned that sitting in silence and stillness was "the better part" that brought them inner peace and a deeper awareness of the mystery of God. Mary may have been familiar with Psalm 46, "Be still, and know that I am God." Martha wanted to make sure they had a nice meal. After all, more than likely this was a special event.

Martha anxiously worked to get a meal together to feed the Lord.

Mary was sitting silently, being fed by the Lord. Jesus said that what she gained by sitting silently and listening calmly could not be taken away from her.

If we can sit still in the Lord's presence like Mary did, then something that can never be taken away from us happens to us too.

Stress is stolen property. Stress doesn't belong to you.

If stress were a gift from God, it would bring you joy.

Does stress bring you joy?

Everywhere we turn, people harp about the stress in their lives. Stress crushes what's lovely in us. We lose who we are and why we're on earth for such a time as this. Try increasing your daily sessions of Quiet Prayer to give the Lord Jesus the freedom to touch you deeply. He will show by His Spirit the one thing that's necessary, the thing that can never be taken from you.

Overcome by Love

KNOWING WE'RE LOVED BY GOD IS ONE THING; living His love through us is another.

Fill yourself with who He is.

It's astonishing how beautiful you are to God. Call Him by His name: *Love.*

Love and your soul are one.

———

Can you love God in the most awful situation?

Can you put an end to words in your vocabulary like: "*I hate* this or that" or "*Why is everything up to me?*" or "*I can't stand* [whatever]."

You and I both realize that God, with all His great promises, didn't promise we'd never suffer. So we must also realize that the Holy Spirit in us does not suffer. That's what Jesus was teaching in the Sermon on the Mount. We're blessed in suffering and hardships because the Holy Spirit empowers us to overcome. (Read the section in this book on the Beatitudes, pages 29–37.)

St. John of the Cross

St. John of the Cross, the sixteenth-century Spanish monk, was thrown into prison in August 1578. His cell was windowless, stifling hot, and no bigger than a public toilet stall. In winter it was unheated and freezing cold. The space was so small the monk couldn't stand erect in it. He was not allowed to wash or change his clothes and was infested with lice. His daily diet was a little bread, a sardine, and water. Dysentery plagued him.

To add to his suffering, his captors were brothers, fellow monks with whom he had lived. They circled his kneeling body daily and whipped his bare back with leather straps; and because of these beatings, John suffered with crippled shoulders for the rest of his life. Half dead, after eleven agonizing months, he escaped.

John later wrote that he was most thankful for those wretched months because they taught him to know God's presence without any sign of Him, without feeling or sensing He was there with him. In his agony he learned the illuminating presence of God was within, and he was at peace.

John wrote most of his famous poems of love and joy in that prison cell. A tortured prisoner with little hope of freedom, he wrote the poems that today are considered among the greatest Spanish poetry ever written. His famous "Dark Night of the Soul" vibrates with love and joy as he describes his soul's passage through the dark night to arrive at an unshakable union with God. Here are two stanzas from the poem translated into English:

On that glad night,

in secret, for no one saw me,

nor did I look at anything,

with no other light or guide

than the one that burned in my heart.

This guided me

more surely than the light of noon

to where he was awaiting me

—him I knew so well—

there in a place where no one appeared.[1]

Relinquishing pain as a gift to God is intensely personal and there's no proven way to do it except by doing it. Words seem so cliché and yet when we focus on the nature of love in us, we don't need words.

Gratitude

JUST LOOK AT US! WE'VE BECOME OVERCOME WITH gratitude!

Gratitude can't occupy the same area of space in your heart as carping and complaining. Which will it be? The truth that emerges from the center of you, from the core of your being, is revealed to you by the One who chose you, and this is worth celebrating. You're possessed by God, you're surrendered and blessed. As His loved child you possess all things. It's time to be grateful.

Look for small things to celebrate. The way your fingers move across the page of this book, the touch of sunlight on your neck, the sound of leaves scraping against the window. Pay attention to the small things and be grateful. "For who has despised the day of small things?" (Zechariah 4:10).

When you purpose in your heart to be grateful, you'll thank and praise the Lord all day long for no reason at all. You'll thank Him for Himself alone, and that's the purest form of gratitude to God.

You no longer need answered prayer to be grateful. You no longer require things work out the way you planned to be grateful (though we rejoice and celebrate these blessings!).

Your personhood now and forever is His, and you can exclaim with a sigh of grateful relief, "It is well with my soul."

The studies made of the effects of gratitude on the overall well-being of a person are unanimously positive. It proves one thing: God created us to be grateful. A thankful heart frees you to love life.

GOD CREATED US

TO BE GRATEFUL.

A THANKFUL

HEART FREES YOU

TO LOVE LIFE.

Nothing opens the gates of heaven like gratitude. In gratitude all things are yours.

> In everything give thanks; for this is the will of God in Christ Jesus for you. (1 Thessalonians 5:18)

> It is good to give thanks unto the LORD,
> And to sing praises to your name, O Most High.
>
> (PSALM 92:1)

> Oh, give thanks to the LORD, for He is good!
> For His mercy endures forever.
>
> (2 CHRONICLES 16:34)

Gratitude has been shown to reduce health complaints too numerous to name, but I've had clients tell me their ulcers have vanished, their headaches are gone, their skin has cleared up, and their bruxism (teeth grinding) has ended. Gratitude must start and end your day.

Deep inside the grateful heart is the treasure of the joy that the whole world seeks.

> For you are a holy people to the LORD your God, and the LORD has chosen you to be a people for Himself, a special treasure above all the peoples who are on the face of the earth. (Deuteronomy 14:2)

> But we have this treasure in earthen vessels, that the excellence of the power may be of God and not of us. (2 Corinthians 4:7)

What do you need to be grateful?

An inmate serving a life sentence in a Texas prison wrote the following poem. He sent it to the prison ministry spearheaded by Benedictine Sister Joan Chittister.

A Thanksgiving Dance

I own nothing but these arms,
So I swing them,
So I clap them.
I have nothing but these legs,
So I lift them in dance.
I have nothing but my own hips,
So I sway them in a trance.
Except I may not even own this body
—but I move.
      Even still I may not say where I go,
      Yet I possess my soul.
"Dance, dance. Dance," said He.
"I am Lord of the Dance" said He.
For all these I give thanks
To the One I owe,
(O my soul dance)
the fact that I exist,
that I breathe and that I know
the One from Whom all blessings flow.[1]

(USED BY PERMISSION)

Judgment

Are you too fat?
Too skinny?
Too old?
Too stupid?
Too clumsy?
Too shy?
Too messy?

THE LIST COULD GO ON. IF YOU JUDGE YOURSELF, you judge others. Judgment is an attitude of the ego, and it's dangerous. It's Lower Self behavior.

Your Higher Self sees beyond your self-centered opinions and casts them aside.

If you can judge others, the way they dress, the cars they buy, how they spend their money, who they marry, and so on, you'll be just as hard on yourself. Nobody really makes the mark, including you. You're too fat, too skinny, too this, too that. Or conversely, you're better than everyone else because you're such a good person. Nobody is better than anyone else and nobody is worse than anyone else. If you can grasp this truth you'll find the portals to God's wisdom swing open.

The judgmental heart is a distorted heart. Quiet Prayer teaches us not to judge. If we judge our ability to sit in stillness and focus on God, we must let go of the idea immediately. Judging relies on your perceptions, opinions, prejudices, fears, family upbringing, cultural standards, peer conditioning, envy, and unexplored mercy terrain in the heart.

Again, to put it simply, nobody is better than anyone else and nobody is worse than anybody else.

Answer the question, *Who am I?*

I'm short. I'm tall. I'm good. I'm decent. I'm bold.
I'm not bold. I'm Jewish. I'm Black. I'm Asian.
I'm old. I'm not short. I'm from New Jersey.

These are mere descriptions and say literally nothing about who you are.

Who am I?
What motivates me?
What's inside me?
Do I know?

Answer the question, *Who am I?*

What do you come up with? A set of outer descriptions, job titles, family origins, gender, and physical attributes?

None of these identify who you are.

You are not where you come from, what you've been through, what your aspirations may be, whether you're rich or poor—none of these descriptions tell who you are.

QUIET

PRAYER

TEACHES

US NOT

TO JUDGE.

You might answer, "I'm a child of God," and that's great, but it's incomplete since we're all His children.

Who you truly are is what's inside you. What makes you tick? What motivates you? What defines you as a spiritual being?

Everything external is temporary. The spiritually alive you will live forever. You're an eternal being. You are born of the Spirit, and it is you as an eternal being that defines who you are. So if you answer, "I am a child of God," can you explain to yourself what that means?

We live in a judgmental culture. We're up against continual pressure to perform well.

It's good if we do well. It's bad if we don't.

We're good if we make the honor roll in school. We're bad if we fail.

We're good if we get a raise at work. We're bad if we get fired.

The levels of guilt and shame we heap on one another are almost inhuman. As God's precious child, examine yourself for the judgmental notions that might be hurting you (and others).

Examine your life for times when you've been judged for what you did or didn't do. Remember the feelings? Anger, shame, and guilt crush the spirit.

After your next period of Quiet Prayer, pile these injustices into an imaginary burlap sack and toss them. Quiet Prayer draws us toward the gates of acceptance, mercy, and renewal. His love covers a multitude of sins (in this instance let's call cruel judgment a sin), both ours and those done to us. It's no sin to fail or to drop out or to give up. It's no sin to lose a contest, fail a test, forget your tickets to the concert. *Stop judging!* It creates a culture of guilt and shame.

A sad reality is that Christians can be the worst, bound in legalism, blasting each other and the world with cruel and ungodly claims on righteousness. The Christian who is quick to judge, to dismiss, and turn his or her back on the wise and merciful voice of the Holy Spirit is unfortunately the model gaining the most attention in the media and the world.

Awake and Alive

GOD IS CALLING YOU TO RISE AND SHINE FOR YOUR light has come—the glory of the Lord has risen upon you (Isaiah 60:1)! Let's no longer be asleep under the dog-eared covers of our sad stories.

The Bible also gives us the reason we're empowered to rise and shine (2 Peter 1:19). Jesus, the Morning Star, has risen *in* us—that is, in our hearts. Through the dynamic, explosive infusion of the Holy Spirit of God in our human spirits, we're awake and alive!

The false self is asleep in the light, dozing uncomfortably in troubles of its own making. Jesus sets us free from our ridiculous selfishness and our senseless efforts to be religious and get God to do what we want Him to do.

Quiet Prayer humbles us. It requires us to hush up and respect stillness.

PART 2

Stillness

Stillness,
the holy act of quieting
the mind and body
    to become one with God
and embraced
in the silence of His voice.
Stillness is the doorway
to knowing God and knowing
yourself in Him.

"BE STILL, AND *KNOW* THAT I AM GOD." (PSALM 46:10)

Rest

Jesus talks to you . . .
You are strongest when you are still.
In quietness and confidence you are strong.
Be still.
I am with you.

    I am the Lord who is exalted above all the earth
and I hold you in the palm of My hand.

    You are safe here and now. This moment
is your safe place, for I am your safe place.

    No need to fight your own battles.
No need to rush out to defend yourself. Your best
  weapons

    are pockets of lint, weightless and wearisome.
No ground is ever gained with feeble, emotional
  attempts

    at conquering that which only I can conquer
  for you.
Don't be afraid of tomorrow when I am beside you.
  The battle is won

    and I am your fierce and undefeated weapon.
The battle is Mine.[1]

    (ISAIAH 30:15; PSALM 46:10–11; 2 CHRONICLES 20:17)

ON A SUNNY FLORIDA MORNING IN JUNE, A MOTHER and her ten-year-old daughter go canoeing on the Manatee River. They paddle leisurely along, basking in the hot sun and the peaceful flow of the river. The water is cool and calm. The air is still. The mother and daughter can see their reflections in the river. When they splash their paddles in the water, their reflections splinter into abstractions.

All is quiet and still until the water is disturbed.

The mother tells the daughter that it's the same with the human soul. It's impossible to see our faces clearly in agitated water, and it's impossible to hear clearly from God with agitated minds. The mother and daughter breathe in the stillness of the morning and the river. The paddles rest at their sides.

————

We look for our faces in the water, but it's difficult when the water's agitated. We must be quiet enough, resting in stillness, before we see clearly just who we are.

Sadly, it can be from a very agitated and distorted mirror within us that we live our devotional lives and lift up our prayers.

Jesus cried out to the storm-raged sea, *"Peace, be still!"* (Mark 4:39).

He says the same to us.

Moses ordered the Israelites to stand and be still when they reached the Red Sea with the Egyptian army hot in pursuit. Trapped with nowhere to run, Moses ordered them to be still.

And Moses said to the people, "Do not be afraid. Stand still, and see the salvation of the Lord, which He will accomplish for you today. For the Egyptians whom you see today, you shall see again no more forever" (Exodus 14:13).

If you need a miracle from God, and who doesn't, use this time to quiet yourself. Return to your Quiet Prayer and be still. Silence all panic and be still. It often happens we aren't still long enough. The prophet Elijah had to learn how to calm himself down in the midst of turmoil if he wanted to hear from God.

Hearing from God and listening to God are at the heart of contemplation.

Elijah

Elijah, called the greatest prophet of the Old Testament, showed that even he—a man who performed amazing miracles, signs, and wonders, and loved God more than life—had a weak side. You can understand how he felt when you consider that Ahab, the king, and his wife, gruesome Jezebel, had annihilated almost all of Israel, and those who were left abandoned God to bow to Baal. Elijah thought every one of God's prophets had been slaughtered. Jezebel sent a hateful death warrant to Elijah threatening he was next.

The Bible says Elijah "feared for his life" and took off running. He ran all the way to Mount Horeb, called the mountain of God. It took him forty days and forty nights without food to get there. He ran on the strength of a little cake and some water an angel had prepared for him. The whole time he was running, his soul was in agony. He thought it was all over, Israel was done for, and he prayed, begging God to let him die. His heart was broken for God. To think all God's prophets were dead and His people had abandoned Him was unbearable for Elijah.

Elijah hid in a cave. God told him to stand on the mountain and He'd pass by him. Elijah stood and waited and suddenly there came a violent wind tearing into the mountainside. The Lord wasn't in the wind. He was silent.

Then there came a shattering earthquake that broke the side of the mountain in pieces. The Lord wasn't in the earthquake. He was silent.

After that, a fierce, raging fire. God wasn't in the fire either. He was silent.

This shocking experience is reminiscent of the day God passed by Moses in the fire on the mountain (Deuteronomy 5:4). The people were so terrified they ran twelve miles away thinking they'd be consumed by the voice of God.

Finally Elijah heard a sound. Like a gentle whisper, like a sound that's not a sound. God's voice. Was it as dramatic as the crashing, deafening storms preceding it? Was it a booming bass like we hear in the God movies? No. It was a still, small voice. One you'd have to be quiet to hear.

This is the same voice we hear in solitude when God speaks to our spirits. A still, small voice.

God sent Elijah back where he came from, comforting him with the news that there were seven thousand of His prophets left in Israel and all was not lost. Elijah wasn't alone. He still had work to do.

You'll notice as you read the story of Elijah in 1 Kings 19

that God never pampered him, never made it easy for him. He didn't sweetly address him at any time, and He gave him the most impossible miracles to perform amid evil, murderous enemies. He treated Elijah like a toughened, grown man of God.

Elijah's story is one to contemplate. Both terrible and beautiful, it's eminently inspiring.

More About Contemplation

THINKING ABOUT ELIJAH AND CONTEMPLATING HIS relationship with God and God's relationship with him is a spiritually rich journey. Elijah was a man completely possessed by the Holy Spirit of God. The Bible is humankind's treasure trove for contemplation.

The contemplative life invites each Christian into its embrace. Sitting quietly in meditation is one part of the contemplative life. Concentrating on the Word of God and the attributes, nature, and deeds of God is a form of contemplation. There are many methods of Bible study, including individual book study, character study, topical study, and the big picture. Rick Warren, pastor of Saddleback Church in Southern California, has written a book giving fifteen methods of Bible study.[1]

Contemplative reading of the Word is similar to Bible study because contemplation is a thinking, discursive process. Quiet Prayer meditation is not a thinking, discursive process. Meditation is nondiscursive.

Orthodox and Catholic Bible reading traditions of the East and West are called *Lectio Divina* (pronounced Lexio Deveena). It means in Latin, "Divine Reading." *Lectio Divina* is an ancient contemplative practice observed today in Catholic, Anglican, and Orthodox traditions. The monastic classical format begins with a slow, deliberate reading of a passage of Scripture, then pausing to reflect on the words, rereading the passage, reflecting again, and then resting with the words for a period of time. Each step is measured by the same number of minutes. You pray for guidance and understanding by the Holy Spirit and then listen to the words with the ears of the heart.

I suggest to you, and to every Christian, to begin contemplative practice with the first of the 2,461 verses in the Psalms and the New Testament Gospel of John (only 879 verses) for contemplation of God's Word. Billy Graham preached that the Bible is the only reality we have and therefore it is worth contemplating the life it brings us.

Consider Quiet Prayer to follow your Bible reading or begin your period of contemplation. To repeat myself, Quiet Prayer does not take the place of your Bible study or your times of vocal prayer and praise. You might want to sit in Quiet Prayer before leaving for church or when you come home from church. Quiet Prayer is *in addition* to your church involvement.

Whether you're dancing and clapping at a rousing Pentecostal conference with jubilant worship and energetic charismatic speakers, or you're hidden away at a Benedictine monastery in total silence, Quiet Prayer goes with you. Baptist, Methodist, Lutheran, Presbyterian, Anglican, Messianic Jew, Independent, all denominations—Quiet Prayer goes with you.

One with love.
One with joy.
One with peace.
One with patience.
One with kindness.

One with goodness.
One with faithfulness.
One with gentleness.
One with self-control.
One with Quiet Prayer.

> The silence
> Holds with its gloved hand
> The wild hawk of the mind.
> —R. S. Thomas

> Choose solitude. Choose stillness.
> Wrap yourself in the presence of God.
> Wait in sublime stillness.
> God draws you
>   into the inner chamber
>   of His love,
> His secret place
>   and your home.

Our deepest human capacity is realized when we meditate, because it's our capacity to be with God, in God, here and now.

—John Main

QUIET PRAYER

IS *IN ADDITION*

TO YOUR

CHURCH

INVOLVEMENT.

Acceptance

WE HAVE BEEN FOCUSING ON STILLNESS WITH GOD the Father, the Creator of the Universe. Now let's consider His coming to you to sit in your presence. You've learned to invite your Higher Self to detach from the world and its many concerns and distractions to sit alone with God. You've begun this personal journey in what may be a completely new method of meditation for you. You've allotted space in your daily routine for silence to focus on Father God and His Son, Jesus Christ, and this is beautiful.

God loves your presence. He enjoys your presence. When you sit in Quiet Prayer, you're met with complete acceptance. In an earlier chapter we talked about letting go and setting aside unforgiveness or grudges. This you do during your short twenty minutes of Quiet Prayer. God is not about to turn His back on you because you're miffed at somebody. For twenty minutes, drop what bothers you. Let it go. Let God deal with the situation as He floods your heart with Himself.

St. Therese of Lisieux wrote in her autobiography that "it's not necessary to be psychologically healed to be a contemplative and close to God."[1] Jesus accepts us no matter what. If you're mad at yourself or even if you're mad at Him, He accepts that too. Allow Him to enter your presence and just sit with Him without words. Allow yourself to be completely accepted. Allow yourself to be free to be who and where you are right now. He accepts you as you are.

IF YOU'RE READY TO ENTER THE PEACE OF GOD IN
silence now for twenty minutes, let's prepare for our third session of Quiet Prayer. I invite you to experience a new aspect
of your practice. Now that you've practiced Quiet Prayer for
a few weeks, and you've focused on simply "being" in Jesus'
presence, let's move on. You've experienced silence on God's
terms, and you've honored yourself and God by consenting
to stillness and wordlessness in His presence. This in itself is
enough to carry you through the rest of your days of meditation.

Sit in a comfortable seated position with your spine as
straight as can be.

Sit alert with intention and take a couple of nice, deep
breaths.

Breathe in the reality of God's presence. Hold your breath for
a few seconds, then release through your mouth slowly and with
intention, feeling all your cares and concerns release into the air.

For the next moments in Quiet Prayer you have no cares
or worries.

Sit very still, a slight smile on your lips, tongue resting
behind your upper front teeth, and allow your breathing to be
easy and even, inhaling and exhaling through your mouth.

Sitting in stillness and at peace, allow yourself to create a
Sacred Purpose for this sit with God. (Further explanation of
Sacred Purpose follows.)

Bring to mind your Sacred Word, which you'll gently use to brush away the thoughts when they start to flutter across your mind.

Set your timer and sound your bell to begin.

Focus all your attention on Jesus, who He is and what He represents to you. Keep returning to your focus when your mind wanders.

When the timer sounds to indicate the session is over, gently ring your bell and return to your day.

Sit quietly for a moment and bring to your mind the Sacred Purpose you chose before your Quiet Prayer. This is the purpose to keep before you the rest of the day.

Sacred Purpose

At this point in your Quiet Prayer practice we're going to add a personal Sacred Purpose, or Intention, at the beginning of the practice. What is your purpose for your Quiet Prayer practice today?

The purpose you select for this practice today will remain with you all day. It will keep you focused and encouraged during the activities before you. If you select your Sacred Purpose at evening, invite it to remain with you until your next session of Quiet Prayer.

Think of the Person of Jesus and you might choose "faithful" or "wisdom" or "peace" for your Sacred Purpose for this particular practice. There's no right or wrong here. When your Sacred

Purpose is clear to you, give it to yourself as a holy gift and prepare to begin your practice.

Change your Sacred Purpose with each practice or keep it as long as it speaks to you. Yesterday the Sacred Purpose may have been courage. Today it's patience. Knowing Jesus as Love may direct your Sacred Purpose to the word *love*.

Decide on your Sacred Purpose during the silent moment just before you close your eyes and enter into your Quiet Prayer.

Breathe deeply and accept this opportunity to quiet your mind.

Be aware of your Sacred Purpose all day. Whenever you react strongly to any experience, draw on your Sacred Purpose to remind you of God's presence. Honor your Sacred Purpose as more than just a nice idea before meditating. When you honor and fully acknowledge this individual Quiet Prayer's purpose, it will remain with you during the entire day and the night.

Six Points to Increase
Your Power of Focus

1. During the day make it a priority to consciously observe what you see, hear, taste, and smell. Don't wait for extremes. Look for the subtlety in the world around you: the scrape of a tree branch against a windowpane, the texture of a macadamia nut in your mouth. The smell of sand. Observe your perception of negative. What makes it negative?

2. What emotions do you associate with your observations? Do you tend to divide things into categories like good and bad? What do you feel when you do this?

3. Be aware of physical sensations. Are you comfortable in your body? Do you tend to grind you teeth, clench your fists, crunch your shoulders? How often during the day do you smile?

4. Listen to your self-talk. What are you thinking about and telling yourself during the waking day? Here's where you'll begin to recognize patterns of thought, both positive and negative. Note when you're being judgmental, critical, or unforgiving. Pleasant or unpleasant feelings are easy to recognize because feelings follow thoughts, and thoughts are what you tell yourself.

5. Preconceived ideas and thoughts can be destructive elements in your quest for personal focus. Your actual behavior in everyday life is a complex network of experience, self-talk, and action. Be present in your thoughts and practice thinking in present tense.

6. An old French proverb says, "To know all is to forgive all." Worth contemplating.

IN THE BOOK *TELLING YOURSELF THE TRUTH*, Dr. William Backus and I stressed the importance of being aware of, and dealing with, our self-talk—the inner monologue of thoughts we engage in 24/7.

We set forth the principles of Cognitive Restructuring, which includes listening to our self-talk (inner monologue) and following with the question of whether or not what we're telling ourselves is true. If, for example, I recognize that I tell myself (with or without words) that I could never write a book on meditation, I pause and ask, is my self-talk true or not? I rustle up the courage to honestly answer my question. If my self-talk is based on misbeliefs and it's not true I can't do something, I challenge that assumption. I could counter with Scripture: "I can do all things through Christ who strengthens me" (Philippians 4:13). The false self-talk must be replaced with the truth—new and honest self-talk. I *replace* the old false self-talk with the truth: "With God all things are possible."

Quiet Prayer meditation helps put you in a state of inner stillness to be able to observe the world around you without bias, prejudice, or preconception. You find yourself better prepared to recognize the difference between opinion and fact.

Breathe deeply while in your Quiet Prayer practice and also when you are not in your Quiet Prayer practice. Accept the opportunity within you to remain quiet. Be aware. Don't judge yourself, anyone, or anything.

Breathe in stillness.

You're a child of God.

Be.

QUIET PRAYER MEDITATION
HELPS PUT YOU IN A STATE
OF INNER STILLNESS TO
BE ABLE TO OBSERVE THE
WORLD AROUND YOU
WITHOUT BIAS, PREJUDICE,
OR PRECONCEPTION.

PART 3

Alive and Aware

HOW ALIVE AND AWARE ARE YOU? QUIET PRAYER practice sharpens your mind and your awareness abilities, and by doing these two exercise moments—Rock Awareness and Leaf Awareness—you'll advance your power of awareness. I do these several times over a period of a couple of months. I hope you'll enjoy them. I do.

Rock Awareness Exercise

Hold a rock in your hand. Any rock. Sit in a quiet place with your rock. Be silent. No music, no outside noise, no intrusions. Set your timer for ten minutes. Take a slow, deep breath and look at your rock.

Feel it in your hand.

Allow it to show itself to you.

Silently describe the rock to yourself: its movement of color, shadows, ridges, and edges.

Is it smooth in your hand or rough?

What does it feel like when you move your fingers slowly and intentionally across its surfaces?

When the timer sounds, set it for another ten minutes. You'll know ten minutes was not enough for you to really see and know the rock in your hand.

Listen to it, smell it, press it against your chest.

What is its temperature?

You aren't personalizing the rock by giving it a name or talking to it like it's a person. It's a rock and nothing else. What can a rock that's just being a rock in your hand mean to you?

Sit with your rock every day for five days. Always set your timer to keep yourself focused. At the end of five days place your rock in a pile of other rocks. Move them around so your rock becomes hidden among the others. Now spread them out (or better yet, have someone else spread them out). The rocks should be spread close together and touching in a haphazard manner, not in a pile. Stand back and without touching any of the rocks, look them over and point out the one that's yours.

This exercise isn't a scientific experiment to discover more of the molecular structure of the rock. It's an experience for you to connect with a simple rock using purpose, attention, and appreciation.

Leaf Awareness Exercise

HERE'S ANOTHER AWARENESS EXERCISE. FIND A leaf. Any leaf. A leaf from a tree or a plant, but one that strikes you as fairly interesting, the kind of leaf you might want to save pressed in a book. Find a quiet place with no interruptions. Sit with your leaf and look at it.

Take a slow, deep breath in and out. Set your timer for ten minutes. Now it's just you and your leaf. Silently ask, what does it look like?

Can you describe it?

What is its texture?

Hold it up to the light. Can you see its veins and striations?

Describe the colors. Are they bold, muted, quiet, loud?

Are the edges of the leaf smooth or spiky?

Does your leaf have a stem?

Hold it between your fingers. Describe it.

This exercise isn't a botanic examination of its composure, but a sensory experience of appreciation and attention. You're not personifying the leaf; you're simply experiencing the leaf for what it is.

After you've spent a few minutes a day with your leaf for five days, toss it into a scattering of other leaves. Can you identify which one is yours?

Believe it or not, feeling, touching, smelling, holding, and examining a single leaf is another step toward knowing yourself.

You might try this exercise with items from your desk drawer or toolbox. You'll never look at them the same again. Focusing for a designated number of minutes to hold and observe an object for what it is can be a revelatory experience. You're opening your awareness to beyond the norm, which helps develop your power of focus in Quiet Prayer and in life itself.

> Work of the eyes is done, now go and do heart work.
> —Rainer Maria Rilke

The poet Rainer Maria Rilke found a pleasant way to pass time watching the faces of the people walking by his place of work, so he used to spend his lunch hours outside the office. One day he wrote in his notebook: "It never occurred to me before how many faces there are. There are multitudes of people but there are many more faces, because each person has several of them."[1]

Prayer shows us the faces we wear. Which is your true face? Your true self? The False Self and the True Self become more distinct as you continue your practice. Seeing ourselves through the eyes of God is quite sobering. Not only do we see ourselves as precious, loved, and cherished, but we see what we have accepted in ourselves that hurts us as well as our callings in the Lord.

Quiet Prayer builds alertness and awareness while quieting the mind's racing thoughts. We've been given the gift of Quiet Prayer as a lifetime practice to still our inner storms and to know God beyond knowing. Put on the face God loves best.

Quiet Prayer Session

The group of five sits quietly waiting to learn the next steps in Quiet Prayer. "Is it ever possible to be successful at meditation?" asks one.

"Define success," I respond.

"Well, I guess success in this case, at least for me, would be to do this thing well, the way it should be done," comes the answer.

"The way it should be done. That would be appropriate for learning the trapeze or doing surgery, but Quiet Prayer isn't a strict regimen of rules," I say. "Quiet Prayer is an invitation to be quiet and sit with God. However, you're a terrific success at Quiet Prayer simply because success is showing up. That's a well-done deed. It's fulfilling 1 John 3:18 where John calls us his little children and says, 'My little children, let us not love in word or in tongue, but in deed and in truth.'"

"So that's success? The deed of showing up?"

I nod my head. "That's being a success at Quiet Prayer. Even the atmosphere becomes lighter when you show up."

—

Some days in Quiet Prayer meditation, your mind clutter interferes more than others, but that has nothing to do with success or nonsuccess. Show up. Be still and know that He is God.

"How do I build up my ability of focus?" asks the one who said last week he was too nervous and jumpy to sit still and meditate on the presence of God. I tell him he's come a long way by proving he's capable of sitting still, and the group agrees with smiles. One gives a small cheer.

I continue: "The first way to build your power of focus is making it a priority to sit with God in Quiet Prayer every day. I suggest, as you know, two sessions a day, perhaps more."

A good schedule to keep is to sit in Quiet Prayer first thing in the morning and again before your evening meal. In these moments you're totally given to God, and He to you.

In time you'll notice much happening within you. Your daily life becomes less driven by what's around you. There's an inner calm and sharper focus that weren't there before. You may not think your focus in Quiet Prayer is valuable, but no matter what level, it is holy and sacred.

Remember Jesus' invitation to cast your cares on Him (1 Peter 5:7), and I'll never forget hearing His voice, "Will you come sit with Me for a while?"

Have you ever considered that God may enjoy your presence? No?

It's time to tell yourself the truth. Time to tell yourself all is well. These moments alone with God are the best moments of your day. During this short, set-apart time you have nothing to do, nothing to worry about, nothing to plan, and absolutely no pressure. You're free to pour yourself into the open heart of God and let Him enjoy you.

One of the reasons for sitting in your Quiet Prayer time first thing in the morning is because you haven't had a chance to get carried away with your day. No phone calls, texts, or emails yet.

The family's still asleep. If you're in a dorm, find a quiet place where there are no interruptions and head there first thing in the morning before your roommates and other dorm mates are up.

"But it's almost impossible for me to even imagine meditating and being quiet first thing in the morning," says one. "I'm usually in a huge rush to get to work. It's chaos."

Another says, "So try getting up earlier."

I like that response.

"Okay," says our busy-morning person. "I suppose I could try setting my alarm a half hour earlier. But I still think it's impossible."

The look on his face tells me he needs encouraging. I look around. I think we all need encouraging. I suggest we pause and think about morning for a few minutes.

"Here's you," I begin, "and here's your morning—"

Morning.

Make it beautiful. Say a soft "good morning" to yourself, to your surroundings, and to Jesus.

You're awake. How lovely to be awake. Roll over in your bed, feel the sheets beneath you, the pillow under your head. Stretch. Breathe. Smile.

No tension. No rush. Place your feet on the floor and wiggle your toes. Wiggle your fingers. Breathe deeply.

This is the day the Lord has made . . . (Psalm 118:24).

Feel your face. Are you squinting? Frowning? Relax your face. Smile. After you go to the bathroom, pour your coffee, tea, or juice, take your Quiet Prayer designated seat. Let's do this together.

QUIET PRAYER PRACTICE #4

FOR THE FINAL PRACTICE IN THIS BOOK WE'LL incorporate body awareness before beginning the practice. You can do this exercise before all your Quiet Prayer sessions if you like. Here's how it works.

Sit in a comfortable upright position with your Bible nearby.

Breathe in slowly and evenly.

Breathe out slowly and evenly.

Feel your body awake and at ease. No tension.

With your eyes closed, still sitting upright, turn your mind to your feet, which rest flat on the floor. No need to move them.

Now turn your attention to your calves.

Follow with your attention on your thighs.

Now bring your attention on your stomach.

(You're not moving. You're mentally paying attention to each part of your body.)

Now bring your attention to your side.

Follow with bringing your attention to your chest, neck, head, and then your face.

Specifically bring your attention to your eyes, your nose, and your mouth.

Lastly, bring your right hand over your heart.

That's it.

The purpose for this peaceful, easy mind-body connection is for the awareness to remain with you during your day.

It helps you to remember to cherish your body, honor it, and take care of it, to recognize and respect it.

Continue now with your Quiet Prayer meditation, aware that your time alone with God in Quiet Prayer is the best time of day. Reach for your Bible and read Psalm 91:1 aloud to yourself.

> He [she] who dwells in the secret place of the Most High
> Shall abide under the shadow of the Almighty . . .

There's the word *abide* again: stays, remains, is permanently fixed. See yourself first thing in your day as permanently fixed to God.

Set your timer. Adjust yourself so you're sitting upright—pelvis, shoulders, and ears in alignment.

Close your eyes.

Here in your set-apart moments with God you don't have to be anywhere.

You don't need a thing.

You have twenty minutes of complete freedom from all bothers and concerns.

All is well.

Sit in stillness.

When thoughts cross your mind, brush them aside with, "Not now."

Silently speak your Sacred Word and rest in the place where you are totally loved and cherished. You're God's child, the apple of His eye (Deuteronomy 32:10).

Right now nothing exists but you and God.

Quiet Prayer at Every
Stage of Life

CAN YOU TEACH OLD DOGS NEW TRICKS? CAN YOU break old habits ranging from how you hold your fork to rising earlier for Quiet Prayer? According to scientific research, there's no age limit on our human ability to learn, change habits, or to concentrate.

It's comforting to know that when we're in our later years we still can change, drop old habits, and experience life afresh. Our lives can be new every morning.

> [The Lord's mercies] are new every morning. Great and beyond measure is Your faithfulness. (Lamentations 3:23 AMP)

Scientific evidence shows us beyond a shadow of doubt that it's possible to teach our brains to follow new pathways at any age. Quiet Prayer accomplishes this. We've barely scratched the surface of the research that's out there, and every day there are sheaves more.

Lasting happiness is God Himself. This we can know at any age—from childhood to old age—as long as we're always on the lookout for new challenges, interests, and, of course, deeper prayer lives.

Research has shown that people who meditate and pray are happier and live longer.

LASTING

HAPPINESS

IS GOD

HIMSELF,

Children do well at meditation also. Sitting still can be a beautiful thing for parents to share with their children. Children do well for about five minutes, and they need an image to concentrate on. It's being still that is the great benefit for the child. The practice has a calming effect all during the day, especially if it's done with regularity.

What's Happening
Around You?

ALIVE AND AWARE BEGINS BY OPENING THE EYES OF
our hearts to what's around us for the subtle and often hidden
blessings. Can you see with the eyes of your heart that God is in
all things? When walking along in a congested, noisy, foreign city,
can you recognize the presence of God in the midst of the chaos?

The Holy Spirit is in you to see with God's eyes, to hear
with His ears, and to follow His guidance with a renewed mind.
Knowing the presence of God from deep within makes it easier
to see Him outwardly. He leads us in spiritual discernment so we
aren't taken up with appearances and sensations.

The contemplative Christian knows God from deep within
and looks within to know His mind and His thoughts. This profound knowing and union with Him isn't something that falls on
us overnight. This is why contemplation is called Bible study, and
Quiet Prayer is called "practice."

The stillness within you invites you to experience more hours
of your day with being alive and aware. Here are some suggestions
to consider:

Focus on one activity at a time.
Carry this skill to your workplace, school, or home
throughout your day.

As your day progresses, stay in the present moment, respecting the present moment you've been given.

The present moment is a gift to be honored in whatever state of mind you're in.

Pause during the day to take some long, slow, deep breaths.

Bring your awareness of God to each breath.

Take off your shoes and stand barefoot for a few minutes on the earth.

Walk barefoot in grass.

Find a place outside to lie on your back and watch the dance of the clouds.

Ponder the brilliant blizzard in a single snowflake.

Listen for the music of the rain.

———

Create a "welcome home" routine for yourself so when you return home after being gone, you can relax in the presence of God and be refreshed. This will take some planning, particularly if you have family, roommates, or animals. Returning home can be as hectic as your day if you don't arrange for moments to rest and breathe. It can be like a kiss from God.

Let returning home be peaceful and rewarding.

When waiting for an appointment, instead of reading an out-of-date magazine or scrolling through your trusty cell phone, try this focus exercise:

With your eyes open and slightly lowered, without moving your head, name three things you can see around you.
When you've done that, sit very still and name three things you can hear around you.
Now go back, and without moving your head, find two different things you see and hear around you.
Finally, look around and find only one thing you see and only one thing you hear.

This easy little focus exercise not only sharpens your mind, it helps your awareness of living in the present moment.

———

Between your Quiet Prayer practice times during the day, pause for a few minutes and check in with yourself.

How are you feeling?

Is any part of your body tense?

Move your head side to side.

Any stiffness or tension?

Do a brief attitude check.

Are you feeling stressed out?

Nervous?

Bored?

Joyous?

Tired?

Recognize your feelings, both emotional and physical.

Honor them.

After taking a long, deep breath in and out, address your feelings and attitudes with gratitude.

This is a good time to speak the Word of God to yourself:

> Yes, I have loved you with an everlasting love;
> Therefore with loving kindness I have drawn you.
>
> (JEREMIAH 31:3)

Quiet Prayer and Your Attention Span

A YOUNG MOTHER HAD BEEN PRACTICING QUIET Prayer faithfully for three months. Her son had a dental appointment so she drove him to the dentist's office and then paused at the door of the lobby. She was struck by a carved wooden sculpture standing against the wall. She stopped to admire it. "Look, son!" she exclaimed. "They've installed a statue in here! Isn't it beautiful?" The surprised boy replied, "Mom, we've been coming here for ages and that statue has always been there. You just didn't notice it."

What about you? How are you doing in the Observation of the World Around You department?

Do you find yourself more aware since you began Quiet Prayer practice?

Are you in the here and now of life or are you waiting for tomorrow?

Are you hanging on to yesterday as if you lost your favorite teddy bear or your wedding ring?

I've got another focus exercise for you. You probably did this one in grade school, but here goes:

Set the timer for ten or twenty seconds and look around the area where you are.

At the sound of the timer, shut your eyes and name as many things as you can remember in the area.

Do it again. This time look around at the colors and shapes in the area.

At the sound of the timer, shut your eyes and name as many colors and shapes as you can remember in the area.

Practice these exercises with intention and focus. They're especially good to practice in waiting rooms. And try your own bedroom or kitchen. You'll be surprised at what you haven't noticed before.

Once you have become accustomed to these exercises as outward experiences, now look within.

What meaning do things carry?

Think about the place where you live—your house, apartment, room, trailer, yurt. If it could talk, what would it say to you? Would it thank you for being such a kind, thoughtful, grateful tenant?

How much space does God take where you live?

Quiet Prayer in a Hurry

I REALIZE YOU'RE BUSY AND YOU'D LIKE TO KNOW how to meditate when you're always in a hurry. Everyone tells me this. Let's listen to the wisdom of managers of large companies. The adage goes like this: "Always find the busiest person to do some urgent task because they're the ones who get things done." I may not have quoted it exactly, but the message is, if you're always in a hurry and you're insanely busy, you're a great candidate for creating time to meditate.

I've learned a rushed schedule is no reason to eliminate time in Quiet Prayer. Any time I spend in Quiet Prayer practice is good. Taking just a few minutes to focus on God's presence in me is better than waiting until I have more time, which is about as realistic as saying I'd go to the moon if I only had more time.

When you've made your Sacred Purpose in the morning, and you're out pursuing your busy day, you may find you need a power-surged spiritual pickup with a quick dose of Quiet Prayer. (Remember your Sacred Purpose? When you wake in the mornings, initiate a Sacred Purpose for your day with just one word: *patience, respect, peace, acceptance, tolerance, love,* and so forth.)

Here's a solution:

1. Gently close your eyes wherever you are and focus your attention on the presence of God, just as you do in regular Quiet Prayer practice.

2. Breathe Jesus into your awareness. Be aware that you are one with Him. He is in you by His Spirit and all is well.

3. Be still. Sit or stand upright and breathe slowly and evenly. Allow your body to release all tension. Know God's presence is in you and you are in His. Stay put until this awareness is very real to you.

4. Before opening your eyes repeat your Sacred Purpose word. It could be *joy* or *patience* or *mercy* or *steadfast* or *peace*. Whatever it is, speak the word silently to yourself and to God. (If you didn't initiate a Sacred Purpose this morning, do it now. No problem.)

These Quick Quiet Prayer sessions throughout the day are great reminders of who you are and who Jesus is in you. These brief moments require you to pull out from your inner being the truth of God's presence, His love for you, and your love for Him.

When you're walking, focus your mind on where you are, your surroundings, the colors, shapes, shadows, and sounds.

Breathe in the air. Humid? Hot? Breezy? Cool? Cold? Windy? Pause to feel it.

What's going on right now where you are? Be there. (Look for sculptures you haven't noticed before.)

You aren't judging or analyzing—you're experiencing.

You're alive!

———

Here's another suggestion to enhance your contemplative life:

Carry at least ten Scripture verses with you at all times.
Refer to them during the day.
Repeat them aloud or silently as you go about your activities.
Here are some recommendations:

It is God who works in you both to will and to do for His good pleasure. (Philippians 2:13)

> This is the word of the LORD to Zerubbabel:
> "Not by might nor by power, but My Spirit,"
> Says the LORD of hosts.
>
> (ZECHARIAH 4:6)

Do not be drunk with wine, in which is dissipation; but be filled with the Spirit. (Ephesians 5:18)

> The LORD has appeared of old to me, saying:
> "Yes, I have loved you with an everlasting love;
> Therefore with lovingkindness I have drawn you."
>   (Jeremiah 31:3)

> Let all the earth fear the LORD;
> Let all the inhabitants of the world stand in awe
>   of Him.
> For He spoke, and it was done;
> He commanded, and it stood fast.
>
> (PSALM 33:8–9)

My voice You shall hear in the morning, O Lord;
In the morning I will direct it to You,
And I will look up.

(PSALM 5:3)

To them God willed to make known what are the riches of the glory of this mystery among the Gentiles: which is Christ in you, the hope of glory. (Colossians 1:27)

For He satisfies the longing soul,
And fills the hungry soul with goodness.

(PSALM 107:9)

(For the Lord your God is a merciful God), He will not forsake you nor destroy you, nor forget the covenant of your fathers which He swore to them. (Deuteronomy 4:31)

Let this mind be in you which was also in Christ Jesus. (Philippians 2:5)

Let your conduct be without covetousness; be content with such things as you have. For He Himself has said, "I will never leave you nor forsake you." (Hebrews 13:5)

But the Helper, the Holy Spirit, whom the Father will send in My name, He will teach you all things, and bring to your remembrance all things that I said to you. (John 14:26)

I indeed baptize you with water unto repentance, but He who is coming after me is mightier than I, whose sandals I am not worthy to carry. He will baptize you with the Holy Spirit and fire. (Matthew 3:11)

Driving: A Contemplative Learns Patience

DRIVING CAN BE A MAMMOTH TEST OF PATIENCE. Father Richard Rohr told how he would lose patience every time he came to a certain stoplight near his monastery. He said it had to be the longest stoplight ever erected. One day as he sat grousing impatiently behind the wheel while waiting at the interminable stoplight, he heard the Lord speak to him: "Will you be any happier on the other side?"

That was the end of Father Rohr's impatience. You might want to think about those words when you face a long stoplight.

Take the opportunity to take some long, slow, deep breaths as you wait for the light to change.

Relax your muscles in your neck and your face.

Pull in your abdominal muscles and make some small circles with your shoulders.

Recite one of the ten Scripture verses you carry with you.

Smile.

The Meditative Prayer Walk

A MEDITATION WALK IS A SNAIL-PACED WALK WITH about three or four seconds between each step. We walk so slowly we almost tip over. Heel to toe, heel to toe. Ever so slowly and deliberately. The idea is to place your focus on the Lord Jesus as well as where you are. If you find yourself thinking about keeping your balance more than anything else, adjust your steps accordingly.

It's a beautiful thing to see a stream of Christian pilgrims all in a row, snaking their way through a monastery garden one halting step at a time. For this reason I like to be at the end so I can appreciate the sense of oneness we all share with the Lord.

You can do your own private Prayer Walk on your patio or in your bedroom. If you have to step sideways to keep your balance, so be it. Just make it *verrrry* slow. Keep your eyes lowered to watch where you're going without turning your head. Hold your hands either behind your back or folded in front of you.

The Meditative Prayer Walk enjoins your Quiet Prayer practice with very slow movements to help recognize and release you from the mad rush and chaos of the world around you, as well as the chaos that may fester within.

Let your soul be calmed as you're tenderly drawn back to the place of peace where you were born to live.

The Silent Retreat

I LOVE A SILENT RETREAT, A PERIOD OF COMPLETE silence for five to ten days or longer.

No talking, radios, cell phones, TV, chit-chat, video chats, tablets, laptops, or Alexa—silence.

At meals you hear only the scraping of forks on plates, the chewing and swallowing of the person next to you, the soft footsteps of a fellow pilgrim.

Sheer heaven.

I love a silent retreat.

If you want to really get to know yourself, try not talking for a week. Spend that week in Quiet Prayer and contemplation. Silence is the language of God and what better way to meet your inner self than through the perfect lens of the Holy Spirit?

Sometimes Christian retreat centers and monasteries offer individual one- and two-day silent retreats for God's children to quiet their souls. There are usually gardens and lovely walkways to wander in, and these heavenly hours alone with Jesus will do more for you than a month at a five-star beach resort.

A nice vacation is fine for relaxing and having fun. These things are important, but if it's "peace that passes understanding" you crave, try a silent retreat with just you, Jesus, the Word of God, nature, and silence.

Most silent retreats I attend include a contemplative speaker, morning and evening periods of group meditation, meals, and, of course, silence. The monastery rooms are adequate and clean (not cold cells with a cot and a candle). In the comfortable and inviting milieu, my cares drop off like feathers in the wind. Retreatants always have the option to attend the church services and Mass if they choose.

Connection with Others

QUIET PRAYER PRACTICE BRINGS OUT FROM WITHIN you a natural concern for others and an awareness of their value, no matter who they are. You'll be more conscious of the words you speak and how you speak them. You'll find that your ability to listen is increased. This is because the Holy Spirit within you is working on your attitudes.

You're aware in a new way of the feelings of others and their right to be respected and heard without judgment. You'll find yourself more understanding and patient with difficult people than before you began your Quiet Prayer practice. Your Lower Self pursuit to be liked, admired, and even adored, has run its course, and you're settling into the humble, compassionate person God is changing you into.

Another benefit I began to notice early on in my Quiet Prayer practice is that people treated me differently. Prickly people became softer in the way they spoke to me. One elderly fellow in one of my classes was a veteran curmudgeon. I'm pretty sure he invented the word. Mean-tempered, unfriendly, rude, and angry, he was no picnic to be around. Everyone avoided him. Nevertheless, I decided he was interesting and that I actually liked him.

By the third class this unapproachable, aged tiger had warmed up to the point where he smiled, shared with the group, cleaned up his adjective-challenged language, and even laughed at my sorry jokes. By the end of the ten-week class, he was friends with everybody. He was still a curmudgeon, mind you, but he was a much nicer curmudgeon, and all because of receiving some kind attention.

God's heart takes over our hearts and a multitude of sins is covered.

Fortitude, Grit, and Determination

Fortitude

Your commitment to Quiet Prayer and growing in your inner life in the Lord requires fortitude. Strength of purpose and courage to surmount distractions and anything that will interfere with your practice are necessary.

Zero in on whatever fortitude God has already put in you and build on it with your whole heart. You're one with God Almighty who loves you and waits for these silent moments in silent prayer with you. The benefits of Quiet Prayer are through the diligent building up of your inner life in God.

Obedience rises on the wings of love. We turn in our Lower Selves to honor our Higher Selves because His love has revolutionized our spirits, souls, and bodies and can now do loving acts through us that we were once too proud to perform.

In the Old Testament God repeats Himself eleven times with the words, "Be strong and of good courage."

In the famous "put on the full armor of God" chapter (Ephesians 6), Paul concluded with, "Finally my brethren, be strong in the Lord and in the power of His might" (v. 10).

Be of good courage, and let us be strong for our people and for the cities of our God. And may the Lord do what is good in His sight. (2 Samuel 10:12)

Then Moses called Joshua and said to him in the sight of all Israel, "Be strong and of good courage." (Deuteronomy 31:7)

Let's think about strength and courage as pertaining to Quiet Prayer. We usually consider strength and fortitude needful for doing hard tasks, conquering devils, or overcoming dangers. I'm proposing here that we consider fortitude necessary to meditate.

The Bible mentions *steadfast* twenty-four times in the New King James Version. Quiet Prayer is a daily commitment and the presence of Jesus in you empowers you to be steadfast in your practice with fortitude and purpose.

Grit and Determination

God gives you the grit to be unwavering and resolute. When you are determined to make Quiet Prayer an important part of your life, God recognizes and honors that determination.

His love strengthens you.

Therefore, my beloved brethren, be steadfast, immovable, always abounding in the work of the Lord, knowing that your labor is not in vain in the Lord. (1 Corinthians 15:58)

Therefore, beloved, looking forward to these things, be diligent to be found by Him in peace, without spot and blameless. (2 Peter 3:14)

It takes grit not to lose heart, my friend.

Men always ought to pray and not lose heart. (Luke 18:1)

Furthermore, the Lord says,

> But My faithfulness and My mercy shall be with him.
> (PSALM 89:24)

Gratitude

THE THANKFUL HEART IS A BIG HEART WITH ITS doors wide open for more of the presence of God. If I can thank Him ten thousand times a day, I've barely touched on the honor He's due. To thank God for Himself alone is the highest praise. Ten thousand times a day, a hundred thousand times a day, perhaps can't begin to express the smallest iota of gratitude He's worthy of.

Can we stop begging Him for things and start thanking Him more?

Thank Him continually. You don't need a reason. The psalmist sang out,

> I will bless the LORD at all times;
> His praise shall continually be in my heart.
>
> (PSALM 32:1)

We can do no less.

Who can challenge our mind-sets like God? He gave the world His only Son through a woman's body. Mary's body had to be totally given to God for such a miracle to take place—not only her body, but her soul and spirit as well. She had to be consumed by the Spirit of God and submitted to His will in every way.

God asks no less of us.

When you sit quietly in submission to God in Quiet Prayer, allow your body to submit as well. Your inner being submits to the knowledge of God's presence, and so does your body. Tension and stiffness will diminish. The more you practice Quiet Prayer, the more you give your cells an opportunity to refresh and renew.

Your body, as well as your soul and spirit, becomes one with God's purposes. In Quiet Prayer your will connects inescapably with the will of God.

His desires become your desires.

What delights Him delights you.

You fall in love with that which brings Him pleasure and you abandon your own selfish desires and old ideas of pleasure.

How are these things possible?

By learning to know Him. Be like Joshua who obeyed God by studying the teachings of the Word and thinking about what he had learned day and night. Knowing, loving, and obeying God opened Joshua's heart for God to prosper him inwardly so he could be a success outwardly in the work that lay ahead (Joshua 1:8).

Take a close look at Philippians 4:8 in the Amplified version of the Bible:

> Finally, believers, whatever is true, whatever is honorable and worthy of respect, whatever is right and confirmed by God's word, whatever is pure and wholesome, whatever is lovely and brings peace, whatever is admirable and of good repute; if there is any excellence, if there is anything worthy of praise, think continually on these things [center your mind on them, and implant them in your heart].

Paul described Jesus Himself! When you see Jesus, you see Philippians 4:8.

He is perfect honesty and all truth.

He is pure—perfect purity.

Think on these things, and like Joshua, learn to know who Jesus is in you.

In Jesus' Sermon on the Mount as we discussed earlier, He makes it known that we are blessed when His pure heart is also our pure heart.

O the bliss of the one with My pure heart . . .

O the bliss of the man or woman whose motives are unpolluted like pure metal with no hint of alloy. This person pays the price to love God fully on His terms and completely submits to His Spirit with clear, open, spiritual eyes, the very eyes that see the face of God.

The King James Version reads like this: "Blessed are the pure in heart, for they shall see God" (Matthew 5:8).

Turn the verse around: Blessed are those who see God for they have pure hearts.

But how, you ask?

For you are the temple of the living God. As God has said: "I will dwell in them and walk among them. I will be their God, and they shall be My people" (2 Corinthians 6:16).

Your heart is a place for God to call home.

The Man Who Raised Jesus

LET'S LOOK AT THE LIFE OF JOSEPH, MARY'S husband and the stepfather to Jesus. He was engaged to Mary and suddenly she showed up pregnant. How on earth could he, a regular guy, accept her pregnancy as a miracle? Such a thing was not natural. Joseph lived in a natural world, same as we do.

Israel hadn't seen a miracle in four hundred years, and Joseph wasn't prepared spiritually to rest in the knowledge that God is not limited by the natural world.

How heartbreaking for Joseph to renounce his marriage to Mary, a true treasure and God's choice to bear His Son. She was now a stranger to him. His hopes and dreams of marriage with her were dashed. The cause of his broken heart? Jesus.

Here's Joseph, a real hero of the faith. God touched him in a dream and told him to marry Mary, told him she was telling the truth. Did Joseph argue it wasn't natural? Did he insist on tradition, Jewish Law, the culture of his people? No. He married Mary.

Joseph had to give up the use of his natural mind in order to see with God's mind. He gave up everything he had been taught to think and believe in order to be one with God's will.

Do you see the need to give up your way of thinking for God's way of thinking? It begins by being willing. Quiet Prayer is perfect for this inner work of choosing God's will over ours. It prepares us because Quiet Prayer itself is consenting to the words, "Be still and know that I am God."

God may show you that your thoughts and ideas are exactly like His. Congratulations. Or, like Joseph, He may have to change your mind.

Or, like Abraham, He may reward you beyond your dreams for giving up, at least in your mind, that which you didn't think you could live without. Abraham, then called Abram, was seventy-five years old when God called him to leave everything and head out for unknown lands. He was at an age when he could be collecting social security and taking up watercolor painting, but he obeyed and left family, friends, country of Haran, and all he was familiar with. He packed up his wife and servants, with no knowledge of where he was taking them, and followed God (Genesis 12).

I have to ask myself, what's something in my life that I don't think I can live without?

Here we are, on this spiritual path that I believe transports us through the mystery walls of the "secret place of the most High" into the very center where we are so secure in our love for the Lord and His love for us that we need nothing else. Everything else is secondary.

Quiet Prayer is surrender. We give up certain times in our active day for solitude. We do this because we're in love.

Brother Lawrence

Brother Lawrence, born in 1645, was assigned as cook in the Discalced Carmelite monastery in Paris, France. While the Thirty Years' War raged in Europe, he toiled, cooking all the meals for the monks every day, running errands, scrubbing pots, tending the garden, washing down the tables, the dishes, and the linens.

He's not known for his faithful and demanding labors, but became well-known for his relationship with Jesus. He reveled in continual communion with God, which he called the "practice of the presence of God."

He said, "Even if I bend to pick up a straw, I do it out of love for God."

It's love that calls to us, leads and guides us, and is at the heart of all we are, for God is love. His home is within the purity of our hearts. (*Oh, the bliss of the one with the pure heart.*)

In Matthew 5:8 Jesus further established that He *looks* for the pure in heart, even longs for the pure in heart, because it's the pure in heart who can see God. Six hundred years earlier the psalmist wrote:

The LORD looked down from heaven upon the children of men, to see if there were any that did understand, and seek God. (Psalm 14:2 KJV)

IT'S LOVE THAT CALLS
TO US, LEADS AND
GUIDES US, AND IS
AT THE HEART OF
ALL WE ARE, FOR
GOD IS LOVE.

Quiet Prayer Session

Five of us sit comfortably in our chairs. We're comfortable with one another, comfortable with the brisk early winter morning. All is cozy and comfortable.

The woman on the end raises a question about meditation. "Is it meditating if I just rest quietly and dreamily listen to Christian music? Is that meditation?"

"That's very relaxing," I agree, "but it's not meditation, it's listening to music."

"I read a book somewhere on meditation and the writer said to sit quietly and imagine something beautiful. He said that was meditation."

I'm glad she brought that up.

"A person's soul can be as bleak as a haunted house, devoid of hardly any of the Holy Spirit, and yet the writer said to sit quietly and imagine something beautiful. He said that's meditation."

"There's certainly nothing wrong with relaxing while imagining something pleasant," I begin. "That technique is widely considered meditation because it's focusing on something while calming the mind. The practice of Quiet Prayer Christian Meditation focuses on God more than on His creation. His presence with us and in us builds a permanent shift to our Higher Self, which can only happen through His Spirit. Quiet Prayer is not another good technique for relaxation and release of inner conflict. Quiet Prayer's sole purpose is to create intimacy with God. The wondrous effects are inevitable."

I see a few smiles. Hear a few sighs. I pray they're getting it.

The woman in the chair beside me speaks up. "My aunt who's been at death's door has begun doing Quiet Prayer. I'm really happy for her, but I have a question. Can Quiet Prayer heal us?"

"I'm happy for your aunt too," I tell her.

The room gives a hearty amen. Big smiles.

"But Quiet Prayer doesn't heal. God heals."

I continue, "Quiet Prayer practice soothes our spirits and calms our minds so our prayers go beyond our emotions and needs, beyond feelings and fear; even beyond shock and despair. God hears our prayers and He answers.

"Jesus had a lot to say about praying and asking in His Name: 'And whatever you ask in My name, that I will do, that the Father may be glorified' John 14:13 for starters.

"I believe unequivocally in the healing power of God. Period. I've placed my will inside the vast chambers of God's will, and I nose-dive right into the ocean of needs around me. Sometimes I carry on like Faust to let Him know how serious things are, but for the most part I'm serene and confident before His throne. God heals."

Two people respond with a warmhearted amen.

"Are you familiar with Psalm 103?" I ask. "David addressed his soul in that psalm, commanding his intellect, emotions, and will to 'bless the Lord.' Here's what he demands of himself:

> Bless the LORD, O my soul;
> And all that is within me, bless His holy name.

He continues with:

> And forget not all His benefits;
> Who forgives all your iniquities,
> Who heals all your diseases.
> Who redeems your life from destruction,
> Who crowns you with lovingkindness
> and tender mercies,
> Who satisfies your mouth with good things,
> So that your youth is renewed like the eagle's.
>
> (vv. 1–5)

"David called out to the depth of his soul to bring what's there to God, who is the fountain of everything good. David also commanded his soul to remember all the benefits God has given the human race.

"If we translate the word *bless* as we did in the section on the Beatitudes earlier, these verses could read, 'O the bliss you can bring God, my soul!'

"If you're like me, you can mouth words like, 'Praise the Lord,' and 'Bless the Lord, O my soul,' but we have to ask, where are those words coming from?

"That's why the first of God's benefits David admonished his soul to remember is forgiveness—'*who forgives all your iniquities.*' God makes it clear to us throughout the Bible that He's a forgiving God. He's more than happy to clean up the haunted house of our soul and fill us with Himself."

A new heart also will I give you, and a new spirit will I put within you; and I will take away the stony heart out of your flesh, and I will give you a heart of flesh. (Ezekiel 36:26 KJV)

"What can be more beautiful than when we give Him all the joy, faith, love, gratitude, honor, peace, delight, and bliss that He gives us? I tell my soul to present to God the bliss He has given me. I tell my soul to add the eternal bliss within me to the eternal bliss of God's."

The man across from me responds in a breathless voice: "When you say *bliss*, that's the exact word for the peace I feel inside. Since I've become a Quiet Prayer meditator I have peace inside me that was never there before. I can say it's blissful for sure."

He gets it.

Miraculous Healings

I've witnessed hundreds of miraculous healings in my years of ministry, but I've never come upon a sure-cut formula for miraculous healing. If there were such a thing, Christians would put the medical profession out of business.

If you want your meditation to have a life-impacting, lasting effect, make Quiet Prayer practice a regular part of your life. It can be a challenge at first, and it can be hard work and take dedication to keep it up, but think of it this way: Suppose Quiet Prayer were a simple, easy-peasy, no-challenges activity. Compare that to basketball and we'd all be instant Michael Jordans on the court. No need for practice. No need for discipline. No need for commitment.

We can feel good that we're part of a historic tradition.

Meditating Christians throughout the ages have blazed the trail so we can follow the same sacred path in Christ. Christian meditation and contemplation has flowed from the caves of the ancient anchorites, through the cloistered monasteries and convents, and into the world of believers today. The desert ammas and abbas dwelled in caves to live their days solidly fixed on Christ. We're surrounded by angels and a great cloud of witnesses:

> Therefore we also, since we are surrounded by so great a cloud of witnesses, let us lay aside every weight, and the sin which so easily ensnares us, and let us run with endurance the race that is set before us. (Hebrews 12:1)

As you already know, in Quiet Prayer we don't ask for anything or intercede in prayer because those applications are for later. The primary purpose is to develop and maintain intimacy with God. The rewards and benefits aren't our primary purpose.

Try not to forget to begin your daily Quiet Prayer sessions with a Sacred Purpose. You'll find it sticking with you all day. It becomes especially powerful in your regular prayer times, particularly intercession.

These are aspects of God deep down in your spirit through His Spirit in you. They need to be continually awakened. Permit the Lord to pull these God-kissed aspects out of you. In this way when you enter intercessory prayer you are more confident and faith-prepared as you send the presence of God to each need.

More Experienced
at Your Practice

When you started your Quiet Prayer practice, it most likely seemed strange to you because you were so accustomed to thoughts, feelings, imagination, images, music, and words in your prayer time. Planning, dreaming, praying out loud, and singing all have a place in your prayer life, but Quiet Prayer is different, as you've found out.

You're more experienced now, and you know it gets better with time. The more you practice Quiet Prayer, the better it gets because the more you practice, the more deeply you fall in love with the Lover of your soul.

Quiet Prayer meditation naturally builds a stronger faith in you by virtue of the fact that you're alone in silence with Jesus, focused on who He is, and regularly contemplating His Word. You're rising up with deeper faith, and deeper faith is the foundation of your peace.

Clarity and Focus

Losing and Misplacing Things

Because you are regularly meditating, the landscape of your world is expanding. You've uncovered beauty in yourself born of the beauty of God. You're more confident. You're more peaceful within. You've become much less self-conscious and full of yourself. You walk lighter. You just may be the most authentic person you know.

Here's a way to exercise your inspiring authenticity. Make a focused choice not to lose anything or misplace anything all day.

No, I'm not kidding. Decide that you'll be aware of where you set things down or where you leave something and be consciously aware of where things belong.

This is a knotty assignment for me. I may be authentic, but I've also been notoriously absentminded. My daughter feared it was terminal. I'd leave my glasses on anything with a surface and forget them there. I'd always misplace my cell phone, and I was sure certain notes to myself, letters, books, and papers came with legs so they could run and hide. If absentmindedness were a sign of high intelligence, I would be Einstein.

God is a God of order and He remembers where He puts things. (Thankfully!) I know He desires us to be orderly too. This exercise helps to focus on what's important to us—keys, glasses, cell phones, shoes, and anything else we tend to misplace. I'm happy to say I'm much better at this these days.

My epiphany came one morning following my Quiet Prayer session while crawling around on the floor looking for my shoes. I had been working on improving clarity and focus in my daily life and suddenly the word *respect* came to me. I bolted upright. *Respect?* Then came the epiphany. Humbly I prayed: "Jesus, forgive me. I don't show respect for what's mine."

Everything that's ours deserves our respect.

Days, weeks, and months practicing these exercises I'm sharing with you have helped me in more ways than one. I began the process of weeding out, organizing, and creating more space. When I honor what's mine I'm alert to where I put those things.

It's quite possible to lose our inner peace when we're running late and we can't find the car keys. Or when we arrive at the concert and don't have the tickets.

Quiet Prayer builds our power of attention and clarity of mind. Regular practice of Quiet Prayer teaches us to be consciously aware of right now. When we live in the now and are aware of where our minds are and what our hands and feet are doing, chances are we won't lose things or misplace them as often.

Clarity and Focus Exercise 1

Try this "one day at a time." Add another day after that. And another. Don't think in terms of weeks. Start slowly. For one twenty-four-hour day do not misplace, lose, or forget a thing. If you have to, write things down. (The car is parked on L4F21.) Make vivid mental notes: I'm setting my coffee cup down on little table in the front room. I'm putting the address of that babysitter in the red box on my desk. I'm remembering to take out my contacts.

QUIET PRAYER

BUILDS OUR

POWER OF

ATTENTION AND

CLARITY OF MIND.

Clarity and Focus Exercise 2

If forgetting names is becoming more common for you, Quiet Prayer practice has been proven to sharpen memory. Be very conscious of names, dates, and where and when things happen. Keep a notebook and write things down, repeat them to yourself. Pray, and the Holy Spirit will give you what you need to sharpen your focus as you surrender your beautiful mind to Him.

Clarity and Focus Exercise 3

This is the most important of the exercises. Choose your favorite translation of the Bible and memorize Scripture. I suggest choosing one translation so you don't confuse yourself. I personally use the New King James Version because I was raised with the King James Version and I'm so familiar with it. To enrich my studies, I use other translations such as the Amplified Bible, the Complete Jewish Bible, the Expanded Bible, and the New Revised Standard Catholic Bible. There are more than five hundred English versions to choose from.

Love your Bible. Know where it is at all times. If you read your Bible on your cell phone or tablet, keep them near you.

Clarity and Focus Exercise 4

Select a verse a week. Psalm 91 will carry you through for the rest of your life. So will Psalm 103, and not to mention the Beatitudes and 1 Corinthians 13. And don't forget Romans 12:1–2.

If you follow these exercises, I think you'll be very pleased at the level of focus you'll reach and continue to reach in your daily life. Much research has been conducted showing that people who engage in general forms of meditation do better on the job than people who don't meditate. The studies show that people who meditate have far better abilities to focus and concentrate.

People who meditate move up the ladder of success quickly because of their abilities of focus and concentration on the job. Also students who meditate get higher grades on tests like the GRE and the SAT than those who don't.

The statistics here refer to general secular forms of meditation. Modern-day Christians have been slow to do their research and discover the miracle-producing power of God that He longs to instill in us through stillness with our focus on Him. Even if there's only a handful of us responding to this call to intimacy with our Lord Jesus, we're a testimony to His eternal power. Free of anxiety and stress, we're who we were born to be.

All sunshine makes a desert.

—Ancient Proverb

Attachments

QUIET PRAYER FREES YOU FROM ATTACHING YOUR happiness to anything other than God. Attachments can be a source of great sorrow because attachments can fail, become lost, or die. Often what we think is love is really a need to control in disguise. I know people who still lament something they broke or lost years ago. It continues to bother them, like an open sore that won't go away.

Some of my unhappiest counseling clients are people who won't let go of something they lost—a job, money, prestige, opportunities, or a relationship broken through betrayal. The one attachment we can trust is our attachment to God Himself.

Letting go of attachments is preached in most Eastern religious meditation practices and in Western secular meditation circles. The theory is that intense attachment to anything—be it position, talent, possessions, or relationships—is a setup for ecstasy and also for despair. Both are out of balance. The idea that's espoused is to keep a calm and even perspective without going overboard either way.

As Christians we, too, are to be acutely aware of extremes in our lives. There's a time to be extremely joyous—a time to celebrate, to jump up and down, throw our arms up in delight. And there's a time to wade in the dark waters of sorrow. The key is to experience all things as who we are in Christ.

QUIET PRAYER

FREES YOU FROM

ATTACHING YOUR

HAPPINESS TO

ANYTHING OTHER

THAN GOD.

There's a great gulf fixed between the way of the Christian and the way of the world. We're in the world but we're not of the world. Jesus prayed to the Father for us: "They are not of the world, just as I am not of the world" (John 17:14), which tells us that you and I are citizens of His kingdom, His invisible kingdom of the Spirit that is also not of this world. ("My kingdom is not of this world" [John 18:36].)

It's only from this understanding that the Christian can begin to fathom how attachments should be thought of and handled.

In approaching the following familiar Scripture verses, we must take off our blinders of denial and spiritually open our eyes to universal truth. Like gravity, these are the natural laws of life.

> To everything there is a season,
> A time for every purpose under heaven:
> A time to be born,
> And a time to die;
> A time to plant,
> And a time to pluck what is planted;
> A time to kill,
> And a time to heal;
> A time to break down,
> And a time to build up;
> A time to weep,
> And a time to laugh;
> A time to mourn,
> And a time to dance;
> A time to cast away stones,

And a time to gather stones;

A time to embrace,

And a time to refrain from embracing;

A time to gain,

And a time to lose;

A time to keep,

And a time to throw away;

A time to tear,

And a time to sew;

A time to keep silence,

And a time to speak;

A time to love,

And a time to hate;

A time of war,

And a time of peace.

(ECCLESIASTES 3:1–8)

Do you detect any emotion in these eight verses? No, they're simple statements of truth. As a Quiet Prayer meditator, contemplate these verses as you read them slowly and deliberately. How do the words make you feel? See if you can identify what emotion they bring up in you. Listen to yourself.

We can spend our entire lives in denial, never admitting to ourselves that nothing remains the same, whether good or bad. These verses state the fact that all human beings must deal with change. Once we Christians are at peace with the facts, we can begin the spiritual work of handling them.

It's the mature Christian who permits himself to be consumed by the Holy Spirit's wisdom within and can both laugh and cry, possess and lose, and stand up in the natural world (feet flat on the floor, spine erect) with absolutely no anxiety.

Losing a loved one is a truly great loss, and I have the deepest compassion for this loss, for I have lost loved ones too. We live in denial that such a thing could happen, but perhaps, and I risk sounding greeting card-ish here, but perhaps by acknowledging its inevitability, we can honor and rejoice with intention the days we're given on earth with our loved ones, cognizant of the *now* in the "time to live."

Attachment can be translated as control. "Things should go my way." "Bad things shouldn't happen to good people." "What's mine stays mine." "You're not as important as I am." This way of thinking belongs in the spiky sphere of the Lower Self. It's a picture of the selfish child. The child wails when his toy is taken from him. The same child thinks nothing of slugging the other child to get the toy back. That's attachment. Control.

To paraphrase 1 Corinthians 13:11: "When I was a child, I was very selfish because a child's world revolves around him or her. I spoke, understood, and thought as a child. Deep spiritual truth escaped me. But now that I'm a big person, a grown-up, Spirit-filled believer in Christ, I'm empowered to maintain peace and balance through all things, good and bad."

The antidote for a need to control is not passivity, it's balance. Consistent Quiet Prayer practice helps bring you there. Recognize the drive to control and name it. Watch for it when it rears its head in your life. You'll know it by a need or urge to possess, to cling to a thing for fear of losing it; by hating change; and by your reactions to breaking or losing something you value. Most of us go through life not doing this important inner work. It's when you can see and name the Lower Self tendencies that you can begin to do the work of letting go and finding balance.

Feelings

SOMETIMES DURING QUIET PRAYER WE'LL FEEL really great. Sometimes we *won't* feel so great. Sometimes we'll feel happy, sometimes we won't feel happy. Sometimes we'll feel bored, jittery, totally at peace, elated, burning with the fire of heaven, teary-eyed, even sprinkled with angel dust. I invite you to dispense with the feelings.

The reason is, on those occasions when the feelings aren't there or you feel rather empty inside, you may be tempted to think something's wrong. You might tell yourself it's not working, you're not connecting with God, or any number of false assumptions. Allow the feelings to fly away during your Quiet Prayer. Feelings come later.

Emotions and feelings are parallel, and we dispense with them in Quiet Prayer. There are many other benefits you'll notice by accomplishing this. In your daily life you'll find not only can you focus better on your work, studies, tasks, conversations, duties, and sports, but your focus is without anxiety or stress! If you were once nervous around strangers, you'll find it much easier now to drop the old feelings accompanying the situation, feelings of anxiety and fear.

Quiet Prayer Christian meditation is the tool for you to practice freedom. After your sessions is the time to observe your feelings. "I feel so peaceful after Quiet Prayer," is a real and fully aware observation.

During your Quiet Prayer, however, you put feelings aside until later. The results of this practice become delightfully evident in your everyday life as you discover that you're better equipped to brush aside anxiety and stress in what once were seriously stressful situations.

Dropping our feelings during Quiet Prayer settles confusion about God's withdrawing His presence from us. We don't learn to recognize God's presence by our feelings. Remember this in your everyday life as well. Sometimes you'll get goose bumps when you sense God's presence, which is wonderful. Be aware that sometimes the goose bumps won't be there, and that doesn't indicate God isn't there.

Emotions are good, but the spiritually mature Christian doesn't depend on them to discern God's will. He or she is acquainted with the invisible realm of God's Spirit and knows His language of silence. He or she knows how to be still and listen for His leading in silence.

When I speak in churches and at Christian conferences, there's usually a long prayer line at the close of the service. People rush up to the podium with needs, hurts, diseases, and any number of problems, and they want prayer. I rely completely on the gifts of the Holy Spirit as I listen to each need and pray over each person. I must be totally given to the Holy Spirit and well accustomed to being given totally to the Holy Spirit to be God's instrument for these people.

Why do I share this? Because if I, for an instant in prayer, bear the slimmest shadow of any of the following, I'd be out of the will of God and available for the demonic realm to intrude and take over my job. I'd give wrong advice, pray all wrong, and do more harm than good.

Here's the list: intrusive emotions, feelings, opinions, biases, homophobia, need for approval, bigotry, pride, lack of compassion, self-centeredness, impatience, lust, discrimination, partiality, doubt, need to control, intolerance, criticism—can you add to this list?

God hears the needs of His people. He answers, and I must be an emptied, obedient friend of God when praying for others. The Holy Spirit does the work, not I.

I don't rely on my feelings or thoughts to know He's here. I know by His invisible hand. God heals; answers needs; inspires a word of wisdom, encouragement, or guidance; and bestows peace to troubled hearts.

Read the benefits listed in Psalm 103:1–5 again. When you pray for people, you'll see the words come alive before your eyes. Many may give their lives to the Lord Jesus for the first time, and that's what happens when you're totally given to the Holy Spirit both inside and out in every area of your life.

Whether or not you're in ministry, take a break and make time to take a close look at what negativity might lurk in your precious heart. See if you're brave enough to recognize any of the issues listed above. With scrupulous care begin to weed out notions and ideas you know have no business taking up space in the heart and mind of a beautiful Christian like yourself.

This can't be done in a day. It takes time to be open enough to recognize these issues, many of which may be your heart's long-term tenants. Remember, God takes us as we are when we come to Him. He works out the kinks and dents in us later.

This inner work needs to be accompanied by a lot of compassion. Confess with a sense of relief rather than shame.

Expectations

IN QUIET PRAYER, AS YOU WELL KNOW, OUR THOUGHTS are brushed aside. We'll never be able to completely erase all thought, but we can remove something else: *expectation*. If we come to Quiet Prayer meditation with the expectation of being swallowed in euphoria or of flying high in the cockpit of glory, we're setting ourselves up for disappointment.

If we come to Quiet Prayer with the expectation of being bored to death, we're also setting ourselves up. Brush your expectations aside and allow yourself to just "be." I've said it before, I know, but I like to repeat myself. Just "be." No expectations, no preconceived notions, no demands, no fears, no emotional investment—nothing except your obedience and consent to the presence of almighty God in silence.

Whatever expectations you might have had of the practice and results of Quiet Prayer, be certain you've dropped them on the wayside alongside the muddy haystacks of success and failure. These are false expectations, and in your everyday life Quiet Prayer meditation teaches you to deal with them alike, honoring them both.

If you view failure as disastrous and success as something great, you inadvertently make yourself a victim of anxiety, fear, stress, self-doubt, worry, suspicion, dishonesty, back-biting, and worse. These remain with you whether you're a failure or a success at whatever your endeavor is.

Consider now a new you who, through Quiet Prayer meditation, has learned how to take the apostle Paul's words to heart and live them:

> Not that I speak in regard to need, for I have learned in whatever state I am, to be content: I know how to be abased, and I know how to abound. Everywhere and in all things I have learned both to be full and to be hungry, both to abound and to suffer need. (Philippians 4:11–12)

Through your daily practice, you're aware that you no longer are looking for God; you're with Him at all times. He's with you, so His presence is a deep, unshakable knowing. You no longer have the need for outer signs telling you what to do or where to go. The signs are within you in your knowing Him. You no longer fall apart when facing what seems outwardly like insurmountable trials.

Do you see the power and confidence that's yours? The power that's clearly stated in Galatians 2:20:

> I have been crucified with Christ; it is no longer I who live, but Christ lives in me; and the life which I now live in the flesh I live by faith in the Son of God, who loved me and gave Himself for me.

John Cassian

John Cassian, the Christian monk who lived AD 360–435, said that love consists in purity of heart alone. He quoted 1 Corinthians 13 and wrote:

> For not to be envious or boastful or arrogant or rude, not to insist on one's own way, not to rejoice in wrong-doing, not to think evil, and so on—what is all this except always to offer to God a perfect and clean heart and to keep it free from all disturbance. For this we must seek solitude. We can't choose growth and contribution in the place of love. Love must be our motivator.[1]

In God's love we lack nothing. Hildegard of Bingen wrote: "God has gifted creation with everything that is necessary . . . Nothing that is necessary for life is lacking."[2]

The urge to pray and be one with God is built into our human DNA. Christians meditate because we believe in the risen Christ, that He lives, and He lives in us. Our sole desire is to know Him as He desires to be known.

> Pure as the finest gold, hard as the granite stone,
> Wholly as crystal clear your spirit must become.
> —Angelus Silesius

The Now (Yes, *That* Again)

QUIET PRAYER IS A LIFETIME PRACTICE THAT GETS better and better as we learn to be still and let go of heaviness that breaks our spirits. We're learning to let go of unwanted distractions. The early Christian monks considered the distractedness of the human mind as the real meaning of original sin. Father Laurence Freeman explains that this is because of our incapacity to pay attention to God in the present moment. Our thoughts and ingrained habits of thinking can go off on a swamp dance without our conscious awareness. It's the present moment that counts.

> But whoever is united with the Lord is one with Him in spirit.
> (1 Corinthians 6:17 NIV)

Quiet Prayer Session

The young man seated by the door raises his hand. "I always begin my day with Quiet Prayer," he tells the group. "That way I'm a lot more centered and open to the Holy Spirit when I pray over my prayer list. I don't just run down the list to get it over with, and I don't spend time explaining how sick someone is or how bad things are when He already knows. Quiet Prayer has taught me to know God's love in a whole new way."

He stops. Turns his head to the wall.

"I'm sorry," he says, wiping his face. "Men aren't supposed to cry."

We wait, accustomed to tears. God's love can turn any of us into sobbing babes. I've done my share of blubbering. It happens especially after we've been practicing Quiet Prayer for some time. When we come to the realization that His love is part of us, inside us glowing and flowing eternally, it can turn a grown man or woman into a gale storm of tears. I call it Tears of Uncontaminated Gratitude.

The young man blows his nose in a tissue. "Jesus is in me and I get it," he says. "I really get it. I've always thought of Him as separate from me, and I never felt good enough—" His voice goes squeaky. In another minute we'll all be in tears.

"I was raised in a religion where we had to earn God's approval," he squeaks into the tissue.

"Right," I say, and I quote something I read by the Jewish philosopher Franz Rosenzweig: "God did not create religion, he created the world."

Hindrances to Quiet Prayer Practice

HOW ARE YOU DOING? IF YOU'VE BEEN KEEPING UP with me in this book, you've come a long way and I wish I could give you a big hug. There are some things to be aware of that I want to share with you to help your practice. Along the upward path of Quiet Prayer you may find yourself blocked. You might be tempted to put off your Quiet Prayer, and then the day goes by and you haven't sat with God. Here's a list of some of the hindrances you may encounter. Recognize them so you can overcome them if they occur.

Restlessness

The intention of Quiet Prayer practice is not to primarily calm our jagged nerves, but to recognize God for who He is. Sitting still doesn't transform us; it's God by His Spirit who does the work in us. Restlessness shouldn't discourage us because Quiet Prayer practice is not about doing everything "right." All of us get restless at times.

Continue to keep your focus on Jesus, breathe slowly and evenly, and reread the Quiet Prayer exercises and instructions in this book.

Sleepiness

Sleepiness is a hindrance to your Quiet Prayer practice because obviously it's difficult to focus when you're feeling sleepy. Sometimes people doze off almost as soon as they close their eyes. It's fine to fall asleep; just bless your sleep and consider it sacred. But know that sleep is not Quiet Prayer.

A solution to sleepiness is quite simple: go lie down. When you're rested and alert, return and sit with God.

The presence of the Lord calms us and draws us into the peaceful spiritual atmosphere of Himself. Don't judge yourself if you fall asleep.

Laziness

Laziness and poor discipline will hinder your Quiet Prayer practice because the lazy person lacking discipline will give up for absence of immediate tangible rewards. Lack of discipline can lead to depression because self-indulgence is futile and painful. Laziness will also keep you from your practice with words such as, "I'll do it tomorrow."

Unforgiveness

Another hindrance is the mind torn up with lack of forgiveness. "How can I face God to be one with Him when I can't forgive?"

Tell yourself: *for the next twenty minutes I'm going to love God just as I am.* No matter who has hurt you, who you've hurt, or what miserable thing has happened to you, let go. Just for these moments alone with God. Breathe. Be free in the presence of God. He understands. Let Him look at you. As you sit still with God who sees you and knows what you've been through, allow yourself to relax knowing there is no judgment and no distance between you and perfect Love. In time you'll accept His love pouring into you and through you and you'll find forgiveness in Him.

Self-Reliance

Depending on yourself to get things done is a hindrance to meditation. We're so accustomed to doing everything with ego effort and the "If not me, then who?" way of thinking. Can you let it go?

Being Overly Active

Thinking we always have to be doing something creates restlessness. We think we need to be actively engaged. We're dissatisfied if we're not busy. If this is deeply ingrained in our psyche, sitting in stillness can seem a waste of time. We want to make something happen, shake the heavens, do something, and it's very difficult to calm down and be still. Any amount of time we give to stillness in Christ is wonderful. Just don't stop.

Trying to Figure Things Out

This is a hindrance because it misses the point. If we conceptualize what's happening as we practice quieting our minds, we're being discursive. Quiet Prayer practice is nondiscursive because we are endeavoring to quiet our minds, not activate them.

The Holy Spirit creates more of Himself in us daily. Whatever you do, don't stop your Quiet Prayer practice. You'll find that you're unable to harbor the old grievances. Anger can no longer control you. When you are one with God you can no longer be hurt by the world.

Whatever you do, don't stop your sessions with God. Try not to let a day go by without meeting Him and sitting with Him in Quiet Prayer. Uniting yourself with Him as you focus on Him alone is a gift from heaven to lift you up above the barbs of the Lower Self and into the permanent wonder and freedom of your flourishing Higher Self.

These hindrances are merely hindrances, and hindrances can be overcome. They're no problem for God. The biggest mistake we can make is to believe it's up to us in our human strength to do the work only God Almighty can do. It's the Spirit of God in us that transforms and opens the floodgates to union with God.

> Oh, love the LORD, all you His saints!
> For the LORD preserves the faithful.
>
> (PSALM 31:23)

The One-Minute Quiet Prayer

NOW THAT WE'VE LOOKED AT SOME HINDRANCES TO maintaining a Quiet Prayer meditation practice, let me introduce something that hardly gives us an excuse: the One-Minute Quiet Prayer.

One minute? Yes.

One minute is better than no minute. Jesus is right there for you at every minute, ready to wrap His Holy Spirit around your spirit and be one with you. Let it happen. Even if just for one minute.

Sit or stand, it doesn't matter.

Keep yourself upright with spine straight.

Close your eyes or keep your gaze lowered to a few feet in front of you.

Take a long, slow breath in with the silent count of "one."

On the outbreath, silently breathe "Jesus."

Breathe in again with a silent "two."

Breathe out with a silent "Jesus."

Repeat this slow breathing in and out until you've reached ten. The main thing is to keep your breathing slow and even. That's it.

You can do this almost anywhere.

What Quiet Prayer Is Not

QUIET PRAYER PRACTICE IS NOT A TIME FOR RUMINAT-*ing, daydreaming, pondering, planning, dreaming, or thinking.* It is not a time to reflect or fall into reverie. Quiet Prayer is a set-apart time to simply be still and know that God is with you and in you.

Quiet Prayer is not experience-driven. During Quiet Prayer we don't wait for something extraordinary to happen. That is for a different kind of prayer.

Episcopal priest Cynthia Bourgeault said in a course I took with her, "Mystical visions, spiritual consolations, and tantaliz-ing insights all come and go regularly on the spiritual path . . . Radiance and grace are no longer extraordinary events, but simply the ordinary atmosphere of the Love you are beginning to indwell. We need to learn to rest in an undivided sphere of perception where our whole life, both inner and outer stay focused."[1]

Quiet Prayer is not about becoming empty-headed. Quiet Prayer is not about emptying; it's about filling ourselves with the reve-lation of God's presence. We realize, as I said earlier, that the self is what we're obsessed with and where most of our prayers are centered. The *me* is *primo importante* in everything in our little worlds. It's for that reason Quiet Prayer seeks to quiet the self, the *me*, the Lower Self, and sit with God in our interior worlds, for it is He who defines our outer worlds.

John the Baptist said, "He must increase and I must decrease" (John 3:30), and that's the purpose of Quiet Prayer.

Quiet Prayer is not therapy. Although there are many psychological benefits, it's not exactly therapy. Psychological blocks, memories, wounds, and fears are known to diminish and heal, but if it's talk therapy you need, do pursue that route; just don't give up your Quiet Prayer meditation.

Will Quiet Prayer reduce your stress levels? Yes. Will Quiet Prayer help lower your blood pressure and help eliminate headaches? Yes. And much more. Still, *Quiet Prayer is not a medical catch-all.*

Quiet Prayer is not self-hypnosis or going into a trance state. In Quiet Prayer we're alert, aware, and focused.

Quiet Prayer Session

The man sitting across from me wants to know if it's okay to tell a joke.

Five of us lean forward.

"Okay," says the grinning pilgrim. "A contemplative Christian, like me these days, goes to a wise old contemplative master and asks if it's okay to start using email."

"Sure," says the wise teacher. "As long as there are no attachments."

I laugh the hardest, of course.

The happy, relaxed atmosphere in the room is a sweet respite from the cares outside our window. A Baptist lady brought chocolate chip macadamia nut cookies. We learn that one of us was born in Canada, so we figure it might qualify the five of us to call ourselves an International Congress of Quiet Prayer Pilgrims or ICQPP. The Baptist lady finds that hysterical.

"May I ask a question?" asks the joke man.

"Of course."

"Why do we call it 'practice'?"

"Ah. Good question," I answer. "As I see it, Quiet Prayer is referred to as practice because it's not goal oriented. For example, if I try to set a goal that today I'm going to stay focused on God for exactly seventy seconds, allowing no interferences, I'm setting myself up with expectations of myself. Quiet Prayer is about our being still so God can work in us. This takes practice. We'll do it all our lives until we breathe in that last nice, deep breath.

"Think of Quiet Prayer practice as a nondiscursive activity because it's engaged in without goals, thought, or intellectual pursuit. Bible study and contemplating the Word of God is discursive in that we're using our mental faculties. In Quiet Prayer we quiet those faculties. That's practice."

Pens twirl on notebooks. Another question, this time from the chocolate chip macadamia nut cookie person: "What's the difference between our Sacred Purpose and a goal?"

Another good question.

"Your Sacred Purpose or Intention is for one session and one day only. You can use the same Sacred Purpose for many sessions, but it's not geared toward achievement. For instance, my Sacred Purpose for today's Quiet Prayer practice, and therefore my whole day, is obedience. One word: *obedience.*

"Don't forget, when you first began your practice several sessions ago, you weren't ready to select a Sacred Purpose because you'd be tempted to fly off with images and thoughts and goals. In today's practice, I'm going to know in my spirit that obedience is a part of me. I'll simply lay my purpose at the foot of the cross and be quiet with it. A goal is a drive to achieve something. In Quiet Prayer you discover you already have everything."

We pause to settle into our hearts, bodies, and minds for Quiet Prayer.

There's a creaking on the wooden steps outside and the door opens. The woman sitting next to the cookie lady lets out a loud gasp.

"Auntie!" she cries, and rushes to the door to embrace the woman.

Much hugging and tears. We all get in on the happiness of the moment and the poor woman is besieged with volleys of kisses, hugs, squeezing of arms, shoulder tapping, and warm, welcoming words. I barely recognized her with her beaming little face and broad smile.

"Is this the same sick aunt I visited?"

"That's me!" exclaims the woman. "I've come for Quiet Prayer."

Our circle of pilgrims now numbers six.

The Scripture reading for today is Ephesians 1:3:

> Blessed be the God and Father of our Lord Jesus Christ, who has blessed us with every spiritual blessing in the heavenly places in Christ.

Six quiet hearts are certain that heavenly places may be right here.

———

We've been together a year now. I'm sitting with the growing group of pilgrims in silence. I'm with the Lord Jesus. I'm in His presence, focused on Him. Suddenly a delicious idea for a movie sneaks across my mind. Then I can't remember the name of a certain actor. Then unexplainably, I think about the two gray whales stuck in the shallow water off the San Gabriel River between Long Beach and Seal Beach, which reminds me of the halibut in Helsinki. And I've got sixteen minutes to go on the timer.

No judging. No good or bad, no right or wrong. No good

day or bad day. I return to my Sacred Word, brush away Helsinki, the whales, and a star on Hollywood Boulevard to focus on Jesus.

The branches outside the window now wear summer's morning dew like a wet covering of puppy hair. There's the sound of a gray dove moaning on the fence. Six pilgrims sit inside a small bare room, breathing in the new day. Our small circle is a portrait of contentment.

One speaks up. "Marie, what has Quiet Prayer given you?"

"Yes, tell us," they all sing out.

It's the best question I've ever been asked.

I consider telling them how tenderly Quiet Prayer brought me to know God so much deeper, how everything has become new, how free, how good, how alive I am, how simple life has become, how I've come to bliss . . .

They stare, waiting for me to say something.

Okay. I'll tell them how the presence of God in Quiet Prayer is an indescribable inner knowing of Jesus' life in me, how I'm conscious of my life as a love event for God 24/7 because I'm His dwelling place, His home, His temple.

I'll tell them how Quiet Prayer has calmed me down and made room for God to heal my soul as well as my body. Quiet Prayer has bored into my brain "Be still, and know that I am God" with its own private neural pathway.

I'll tell them Quiet Prayer taught me that if there are times when God seems at a distance and nowhere around, He's always there.

I'll tell them I've learned to be at peace like Paul who wrote, "I have learned in whatsoever state I am therewith to be content" (Philippians 4:11 KJV).

I'll tell them how I enjoy the process of Quiet Prayer, how I love knowing all is well no matter what.

The faithful group of pilgrims wait patiently. I realize they want to know what we all want to know. Why are we alive? How can we live blessed lives?

A strong wind rattles the window.

Benefits of Quiet Prayer

THE SCIENTIFICALLY PROVEN BENEFITS OF MEDITATION in general are significant, but the benefits of Christian meditation even exceed those methods of meditation that aren't founded on the traditions of the ancient fathers and mothers of the Christian faith. We practice Quiet Prayer to draw into a deeper relationship with Jesus Christ and the benefits come to us as sublime discoveries.

Here are some of the benefits of regularly practicing Quiet Prayer as we know it today:

Quiet Prayer Meditation

- brings a greater awareness of God within.
- increases feelings of compassion and decreases worry.
- decreases feelings of loneliness, fear, and loss.
- produces a sense of holy confidence.
- increases self-esteem and awareness of being loved.
- creates courage with awareness that fear is not to be feared.
- produces the ability to let go of mental traps and misbeliefs.
- opens the way to freedom from past learning and mindlessness.
- heals the damaged soul.
- brings freedom to love.
- brings freedom from the dominance of the ego.
- produces a deeper passion for loving and enjoying God.
- helps release the heart to communicate with God and not the mind only.

- decreases depression and regulates mood anxiety disorders.
- reduces stress.
- helps reduce symptoms of panic disorder.
- increases gray matter concentration in the brain involved in learning and memory, regulating emotions, developing a sense of self, and having a clearer perspective.
- enlarges the hippocampal and frontal volume of the brain's gray matter.
- enhances the ability to generate gamma waves in the brain.
- helps reduce alcohol and substance abuse.
- improves focus, attention, and ability to work under stress.
- improves information processing and decision making.
- helps with pain management.
- helps manage ADHD.
- increases ability to stay focused through distractions.
- improves rapid memory recall.
- improves visual spatial processing and working memory.
- reduces risk of heart diseases and stroke.
- reduces blood pressure.
- decreases inflammatory disorders.
- decreases cellular level inflammation.
- helps prevent premenstrual syndrome and menopausal symptoms.
- reduces risk of Alzheimer's and premature death.
- helps manage heart rate and respiratory rate.
- helps relate to and excel in the surrounding world with pure-hearted compassion and clearer ability for discernment.

Acknowledgments

Loving gratitude to Father Thomas Keating, a founding father of the Centering Prayer movement, who was good enough to give me his generous advice for this book and encourage me in its writing when we met privately in the library of the St. Benedict Abbey in Snowmass, Colorado, in the winter of 2016, two years before he died. His blessing on this work has born joy and profound humility in me. He suggested the title should be "The Prayer of Consent," which is what meditation is for the Christian: consent to all God is. "Christian meditation is a prayer of consent," he said. "It's an act of the will expressing acceptance to giving oneself to God."

Endless gratitude to my brilliantly talented editor Janene MacIvor and designer Mallory Collins, whose skill and genius turned my manuscript into a work of art.

Thanks to Pastors Che and Sue Ahn of HRock Church and HIM ministries of Pasadena, California. The years of being a part of HIM has been a source of encouragement and inspiration.

Thanks to my fellow pilgrims traveling the path of Quiet Prayer all over the world, especially my personal prayer partners whose prayers for me and this book bless its pages: Cynthia Schlosser, Corrine Jordan, Christa Chapian, Claire Montenu,

Harold Bead, Kayla and Jim Rogers, Tim Placid, Renee Jensen, and most of all and always, Mario Lombardo.

Lastly, it's to publisher Joel Kneedler, to whom I owe my deepest gratitude for so quickly catching the vision for *Quiet Prayer* and for believing in me. I'm blessed beyond measure.

Notes

Introduction

1. St. Teresa of Avila, *The Autobiography of St. Teresa of Avila* (Mineola, New York: Dover Publications, 2010).

Quiet Prayer Practice #1

1. The Monks of New Skete, *In the Spirit of Happiness* (New York: Little Brown and Company, 2000).
2. John Cassian, *Conferences and Institutes*, trans. E.C.S. Gibson, *Nicene and Post Nicene Fathers*, second series, Grand Rapids, MI: Eerdsman, 1982).
3. Rainer Maria Rilke, *Rilke's Book of Hours: Love Poems to God*, trans. Anita Barrows and Joanna Macy (New York, NY: Riverhead Books, 2005), public domain.

The Higher and Lower Self

1. Antony the Great, *The Letters of St. Antony,* trans Dewas Chity (S:G Press, 1977).
2. Wyatt North, trans., *The Life and Prayers of St. Antony of Padua* (Createspace Independent Publisher, 2012).

More About Our Ancestors

1. Louis Bouyer, *Women Mystics* (San Francisco: Ignatius Press, 1993).
2. Bouyer, *Women Mystics*.

Your Brain

1. Rick Hanson, www.rickhanson.net; https://www.rickhanson.net
/calendar/taking-in-the-good-5/.

Overcome by Love

1. Kieran Kavanaugh, OCD, Ed., *John of the Cross Selected Readings,
Classics of Western Spirituality* (New York, NY: Paulist Press, 1987).

Gratitude

1. William Backus and Marie Chapian, *Telling Yourself the Truth*
(Minneapolis, MN: Bethany House, 2000), used by permission.

Rest

1. Marie Chapian, *Talk to Me, Jesus* (Broadstreet, 2016), used by
permission.

More About Contemplation

1. Rick Warren, *Bible Study Methods* (Grand Rapids, MI: Zondervan,
2006).

Acceptance

1. Brother Lawrence, *The Practice of the Presence of God* (New
Kensington, PA: Whittaker House), 15068.

Leaf Awareness Exercise

1. Rainer Maria Rilke, *From the Notebooks of Malte Laurids Brigge*,
Edited and Translated by Stephen Mitchell.

Expectations

1. John Cassian, *The Monks of New Skete* (New York: Little Brown and Company, 1999).
2. Maddox Fiona, *Hildegard of Bengen, a Woman of Her Age* (New York, NY: Faber & Faber, 2013).

What Quiet Prayer Is Not

1. Cynthia Bourgeault, *Centering Prayer and Inner Awakening* (Latham, MD: Cowley Publications, 2004).

About the Author

Marie Chapian, PhD, MFA, is an evangelical contemplative Christian and *New York Times* bestselling author of more than thirty books. Marie is perhaps best known for her *Talk to Me, Jesus* devotional books and her #1 bestselling *Tell Yourself the Truth*. Her own private meditation practice led her to search the history of Christian meditation from biblical times to modern. Her studies took her to ancient writings of Christian saints, mystics, theologians, and historians. Marie lives and teaches in Southern California and travels yearly to monasteries and convents across the country for periods of silence and Quiet Prayer.